# 25 TOP CLASSIC ROCK SONGS

MW00564339

## TAB+ = TAB + TONE + TECHNIQUE

This is not your typical guitar tab book. In the new *Tab+* series from Hal Leonard, we provide you guidance on how to capture the guitar tones for each song as well as tips and advice on the techniques used to play the songs.

Where possible, we've confirmed the gear used on the original recordings via new and previously published interviews with the guitarists, producers, and/or engineers. Then we make general recommendations on how to achieve a similar tone, based on that info.

Some of the songs herein will be easy to play even for advanced beginner players, whereas others present a much greater challenge. In either case, we've identified key techniques in each song that should help you learn the song with greater ease.

ISBN 978-1-4768-1343-1

HAL•LEONARD®
CORPORATION

7777 W. BLUEMOUND RD. P.O. BOX 13819 MILWAUKEE, WI 53213

Visit Hal Leonard Online at
**www.halleonard.com**

# 25 TOP CLASSIC ROCK SONGS

# PERFORMANCE NOTES TAB. TONE. TECHNIQUE.
*By Michael Mueller*

## "ADDICTED TO LOVE"
*Robert Palmer*

Best known for its iconic MTV music video featuring a band of Patrick Nagel–inspired models, Robert Palmer's 1985 hit "Addicted to Love" is otherwise a fairly straightforward power-chord rocker but with a killer one-take guitar solo courtesy of session man Eddie Martinez.

### TONE

In an interview with *Guitar Player* magazine (February 2004), Martinez said he used a Hamer Prototype outfitted with what he calls a "triple-coil pickup," which allowed him to get humbucking or single-coil sounds. It was fed into a non–master volume late-1970s Marshall head accompanied by a Marshall 4x12 cab loaded with 25-watt Celestion Greenbacks. As for settings, Martinez says, "I ran the volume at around eight or nine, because if you cranked that amp you'd lose a little definition. I didn't max out the bass—I let the mids handle the low end of the sound—and I ran the treble at just over halfway." For the solo, Martinez used a ProCo Rat for added gain.

You can cop the tone using a humbucker-equipped guitar—be it Les Paul or "super-Strat" style—through the distortion channel on your amp with the gain set fairly high, or via the use of a distortion pedal. Either way, keep the bass setting down, so it doesn't muddy up the frequency spectrum for the song's signature bass line.

### TECHNIQUE

It doesn't get much simpler than the power chord-driven rhythm part, so let's get straight to the brief but perfect solo, which Martinez laid down in just one late-night take! Using slow, gradual bends and the bluesy rub of the minor 3rd (C) in the A Mixolydian context, Martinez creates anticipatory, almost tease-like, tension that goes a long way in integrating the seductive groove of the tune. For the pinch harmonics in bars 5–6, you'll want the harmonic that sounds one octave higher than the fretted pitch in every case except the downbeat of bar 7, which sounds a 5th higher. You can achieve these different harmonic pitches by moving your attack up or down the string. For example, on an EMG-equipped Fender Strat, I was able to reliably coax the octave harmonic by attacking the G string between the neck and middle pickups, and then the one a 5th higher directly over the neck pickup. Depending on the scale of your guitar's neck, these positions will vary, so use your ears.

## "AFTER MIDNIGHT"
*Eric Clapton*

"Clapton Is God" might be the famous graffiti scrawl, but "King Midas" may have been more apropos for that time in the late 1960s, as everything Clapton touched seem to turn to gold. The Yardbirds, John Mayall's Bluesbreakers, Cream, Blind Faith, Derek & The Dominos, and of course, a burgeoning solo career. "After Midnight," Clapton's first J.J. Cale cover and solo hit, appears on his 1970 self-titled debut.

### TONE

Clapton built his reputation for amazing tones in the 1960s playing an assortment of now-legendary Gibson guitars, including a 1960 Les Paul ("Beano"), a 1964 ES-335 (as heard on "Crossroads"), and the "woman tone"–generating 1964 SG (aka, The Fool). But in 1967, he would purchase a two-tone sunburst 1956 Fender Stratocaster with a maple fretboard, which would later become known as "Brownie" and become his weapon of choice not only for "Layla" but also a good portion of his self-titled debut, including "After Midnight." Clapton paired Brownie with a 1950s Fender Champ (tweed) he got from Delaney Bramlett.

To cop the tone, just plug a Strat into a Fender tube amp and go. One caveat: Though the Fender Champ has a *monster* tone in the studio, it's not easy to use in a live setting, due to its low power and small speaker. You might rather use a slightly more powerful Fender tweed amp like a Tweed Deluxe or a Bassman—or if you've got the scratch, check out Clapton's signature line of Fender amps. Be sure to dial in just a little of that natural tube overdrive sound and use the combination of the bridge and middle pickups.

### TECHNIQUE

For a rock classic, "After Midnight" features a rather funk-fueled riff. Featuring 16th-note syncopation and chord stabs/ accents on the upbeats, this one lies in a loose yet steady pick-hand attack. If you examine the main riff, you'll see quite a few hammer-on and pull-off embellishments. Don't worry so much about hitting the right embellishment in the right measure. Instead, focus on the *basic rhythm*, which is best represented in measure 6 of the Intro. Keep your pick hand moving in a constant 16th-note up-and-down motion, striking the chords only on the indicated subdivisions. Once you're comfortable with the rhythm, work the hammer-ons and pull-offs into the mix.

# "ANOTHER BRICK IN THE WALL, PART 2"
## *Pink Floyd*

Guitarist David Gilmour has become synonymous with the phrase "play with feel," and listening to his solo in "Another Brick in the Wall (Part 2)," it's no surprise. With his fluid pentatonic licks and phrasing aided by precise injections of the melodic 9th and vocal-like over-bends, Gilmour's lines soar more than high enough to clear any wall.

## TONE

For the recording of *The Wall*, Gilmour primarily used his famous Black Strat. However, on this tune, he opted for his equally famous 1954 #0001 Strat for the rhythm parts, recorded direct. For the solo, Gilmour used a P-90 "soapbar"–loaded 1955 Gibson Les Paul goldtop set on the neck pickup. The P-90 has a unique sound—brighter than a humbucker but not as snappy as a typical single-coil—so if you don't have a P-90–equipped axe and are faced with the choice of a humbucker or single-coil, try the latter with the tone control rolled down slightly.

Gilmour recorded the rhythm parts direct to tape—no amps. For the solo, he also ran a clean tone direct, but then re-amped the signal through the Mesa/Boogie for the overdrive portion of the sound. If desired, you can achieve a similar effect by using a Y-cord into two amps—one set clean, the other distorted—making sure to strike a good balance between the two signals. More simply, you can just use an overdrive pedal (easy on the gain setting) through a clean tube amp. Use a compressor (if you have one), to help smooth out the snappy attack necessary to cop the tone.

## TECHNIQUE

For a prog-rock band, "Another Brick in the Wall (Part 2)" is a fairly funky outing. The minor and major chord voicings are straightforward and simple, but the 16th-note syncopations present a rhythmic workout. Be sure to count your subdivisions ("1-ee-and-uh, 2-ee-and-uh," etc.)

Based in D minor pentatonic, Gilmour's solo is rife with cleverly employed soloing devices. The obvious challenge here is Gilmour's formidable overbends and multi-bends, as he wastes no time in executing a whopping two-step bend at the end of bar 2. But the real string-breaker comes bar 10, where Gilmour—with just one pick attack—moves between whole-step, two-step, and two-and-a-half-step bends. Whew! Fret the initial note with your ring finger and use your middle and index fingers to help push those killer bends.

# "AQUALUNG"
## *Jethro Tull*

In the world of rock guitar—and even its little subdivision of prog-rock—Jethro Tull guitarist Martin Barre has never quite received the accolades of which he is deserving. Still, his Celtic folk–influenced compositions and rather economical approach—particularly by prog-rock standards—have produced some of the most memorable rock tunes of all time, including "Aqualung," which features a riff for the ages and an impressive solo, to boot.

## TONE

Inspired by Leslie West of Mountain, Barre purchased a 1958 Gibson Les Paul Junior and used it for the *Aqualung* sessions. He played through Hiwatt heads and 4x12 cabs, with a Hornby Skewes Treble Booster—his "secret weapon"—in line to give the Hiwatt an extra bit of kick. Unfortunately, the Hornby Skewes picked up radio waves quite well, so as Barre has stated on a few occasions, "Any gig within a mile of a radio station was a disaster."

The LP Junior was equipped with a P-90 pickup, which tonally lies somewhere between a single-coil and a humbucker. If you don't have P-90s, a humbucker-equipped guitar will serve you well. If it's a Les Paul-style guitar, give the amp EQ a bit more treble boost to overcome the "darkness" of the tone.

## TECHNIQUE

The main riff of Aqualung is in G minor—a G blues scale, actually—but then Barre takes it on an atonal journey via Db, Eb, and F triads and some insistent single-note lines that cleverly resolve to G. Once you get the feel for the rhythms, it's pretty simple.

Barre's solo thoroughly explores the G minor pentatonic scale in all five positions across the neck. If you're not familiar with all five pentatonic shapes and how they connect, you may wish to revisit them prior to tackling the solo.

# "BEAT IT"
*Michael Jackson*

When recording Michael Jackson's *Thriller*, producer Quincy Jones wanted to help Jackson attain some crossover success, so he decided to give "Beat It" an edgy rock vibe. First, he brought in Steve Lukather—one of the greatest session players of the past 35 years—to record all the guitar parts. Then, when he wanted something a little more, he recruited Eddie Van Halen to do the solo—mission accomplished!

## TONE

To get that rock sound, Lukather recorded the main riff using his cherished 1959 Gibson Les Paul through a screaming Marshall, but Jones said it was too much, so instead he brought in a Fender Princeton and redid the tracks, and that's what made the cut. Van Halen's solo, which he recorded in his own studio, was almost certainly cut with one of his own "Frankenstein" Strats with a humbucker in the bridge into a modded Marshall plexi. But if you listen closely, you'll note that it's not quite Ed's classic "brown sound." When Quincy Jones got the tape back from Ed, he decided that it too was a little too rough, so he had Lukather smooth it out in post-production.

Since you'll need a whammy bar for the solo, your best bet for playing this tune is a "Super-Strat" with a humbucker in the bridge through a Marshall-style amp, with the gain set just moderately. Then for the solo, use an overdrive pedal (e.g., Tube Screamer) on the solo for the extra juice needed to coax the tapped harmonics and to smooth out those legato and tapping lines.

## TECHNIQUE

The Guitar Solo is just filled with signature Van Halen-isms: whammy bar dives, tapping, tapped harmonics, tremolo picking, and more than enough to fill a couple of pages of lessons, much less this small space. Here are a couple of tips to help you more easily pull this one off. First, for the initial divebomb, start either with an open G or the fretted B (4th fret), so you don't have to incorporate the full step bend as notated. For the tapped harmonics that follow (bar 2), be sure to tap *directly* onto the fretwire to sound them properly. Finally, for the tapping parts in general, Eddie uses his index finger for tapping while tucking his pick in the joints of his middle finger. You may find it much easier to simply use your middle finger for the tapped notes while holding your pick as usual between your thumb and index fingers.


# "BROWN SUGAR"
*Rolling Stones*

With "Brown Sugar," from the Rolling Stones' 1971 release *Sticky Fingers*, guitarist Keith Richards perfected for all time not only the greatest classic rock rhythm guitar *sound* ever laid to tape but also the now-ubiquitous I–IV rhythm approach that has become synonymous with Richards's name. Let's take a look at how he did it!

## TONE

Though he's best known for wielding his cherished 1952 butterscotch Fender Tele, Keef actually used a Gibson SG (though no less an expert than George Gruhn argues it was a Dan Armstrong Plexi) to record this classic riff. For amplification, engineer Jimmy Johnson recalls that both Richards and Mick Taylor brought in Fender Twin-Reverbs, and Keith's was recorded "wide open," which gives the track its loudness and slight breakup.

To cop the sound, you can use an SG or similarly humbucker-equipped guitar, or even a Telecaster-style instrument. Use the middle setting on your pickup selector, engaging both the neck and bridge pickups. For the amp, a low-watt tube amp turned all the way up on the clean channel may be your best bet. Alternatively, if you can't work at the high volume necessary to produce that power-tube breakup, place an overdrive pedal with the Drive or Gain set pretty low. In typical Stonesian austerity, the only effect you'll need is a touch of reverb.

## TECHNIQUE

Although you *can* play the riff in standard tuning, using just strings 4–2, retuning to open G and making sure to include the chord roots on the 5th string will go a long way in re-creating Keef's *huge* sound. But if you prefer to stay in standard tuning, use the aforementioned approach of sticking to strings 4–2 for the I–IV changes of the main riff, then switch to the Chuck Berry–style root/5th-root/6th boogie rhythm style during the Verse.

# "CHINA GROVE"

*Doobie Brothers*

By the time the Doobie Brothers released *The Captain and Me* in 1973, the band had already established itself as a certified rock outfit, but it was Tom Johnston's hard-rockin' "pow-pow" riff in "China Grove" that provided the band its most timeless track.

## TONE

Johnston cranked out this gain-drenched doozy using a Gibson SG Standard, and played through either a Fender Bandmaster (tweed) or a 4x10 Bassman. Regardless of which amp he used (he couldn't recall during an interview with *Vintage Guitar*), the amp was cranked to get that mammoth buzzsaw sound. An Echoplex was used to generate the quarter-note delay heard in the intro and its later reprise. The echo is off during the verses.

You can use any axe with a humbucking pickup in the bridge position (Johnston was using PRS guitars on tours of late). If you can generate amp distortion through a tweed-style amp, you're golden, but you can also use a distortion pedal—just be careful not to venture into "heavy metal" saturation levels. For the delay, any standard delay pedal will work. The song's tempo is 142 bpm, so set your rate to about 420 ms, with the frequency set to two repeats.

## TECHNIQUE

In order to give this riff justice, you really need to dig in and hit those chords hard, which means you'll likewise need effective fret-hand muting for the scratches. Between the chord stabs, simply release just enough pressure on the strings to deaden them, but be sure to maintain enough pressure that you don't sound any natural harmonics. During the pre-chorus, chorus and bridge sections, Johnston and Simmons play rather complementary and similar rhythm parts; if you're going to attack this one as a single guitarist, follow Gtr. 1's part throughout.


# "DOMINO"

*Van Morrison*

Recorded at A&R Recording on New York City's legendary 48th Street, in 1970, *His Band and Street Choir* was Van Morrison's follow-up to his hit album *Moondance*. The album's lead track, "Domino," featuring guitarist John Platania, would also be its biggest hit and an all-time rock classic.

## TONE

Platania played the snappy R&B-influenced main riff on his 1964 Fender Strat, with the pickup selector set to the "in-between" position combining the middle and bridge pickups, and plugged into a Fender Twin-Reverb that was sitting in A&R Studios. Though his '64 Strat originally had a 3-way switch, Platania installed a 5-way, though he doesn't recall when he did it, so it's possible that he just "wedged" the 3-way into that so-called "out-of-phase" position. The tone in this tune is so identifiable that you'll certainly want to use a Strat, or similarly single-coil-equipped guitar, with the same pickup setting, through a pristinely clean amp. Aside from the reverb, Platania says he used no pedals or effects, keeping with Van Morrison's "keep it simple" ethos.

## TECHNIQUE

In Platania's words, playing this tune is "all about the riff." It's an ear-grabbing affair that bounces between a 1st-inversion A major triad and two D triads—a 1st-inversion D shape at the 10th fret and a D6 at the 7th fret. The keys to execution are the pull-offs (and occasional grace-note hammers) on the A chord (executed with your fret hand's pinky) and the funky, percussive muted stabs on beats 2 and 4. The I–IV (A–D) progression takes up pretty much the whole tune, with all sorts of rhythmic scratches and syncopations. It's not so important to play every measure note-for-note during the verses and choruses as it is to just *groove* on it.

# "DREAM ON"
## *Aerosmith*

"Dream On," featuring the classic Steven Tyler–penned piano riff, was first released on the band's eponymously titled 1973 debut, but it was the 1976 re-release, along with the raw riffin' of guitarists Joe Perry and Brad Whitford on tunes like "Walk This Way" and "Sweet Emotion," that helped catapult Aerosmith to superstardom.

## TONE

Perry and Whitford have used myriad guitar-amp combinations through the years, but—especially in the early days—the quintessential Aerosmith guitar sound was Les Pauls through Marshalls, and that's likely what we're hearing on this track. The main riff (piano) is doubled by a clean-toned (though not a pristine clean) electric guitar. To get that clean tone, you'll want to have an overdriven sound dialed in on a warm tube amp and then turn your guitar's bridge-position humbucker volume knob down until you have the desired tone. In addition, you'll want to use a somewhat light attack on the piano riff to aid in getting the clean tone, but then pick or pluck a little harder when you want a little breakup, such as on the alternating D♭–C single-note motif and subsequent legato lick that follows the piano riff.

## TECHNIQUE

The best way to approach the pianistic main riff is via hybrid picking, where you play the notes on the 3rd string with your pick, plucking the notes on the top two strings with your middle and ring fingers. To make the change from the Dm7♭5 to Dbmaj7♯11 in measure 2, your fret hand's index and middle fingers will slide back one fret, while the C note in the bass remains stationary. You may either keep your ring finger on that note and use a good stretch or you can switch to your pinky finger to fret the C, as long as you can do it seamlessly and cleanly.

The fills heard throughout the tune are drawn primarily from the minor pentatonic scale using what are likely familiar fingerings. The way Joe Perry makes these otherwise stock lines his own, however, is through his rhythmic and dynamic treatment. For instance, check out the syncopated walk down the F minor pentatonic/blues scale in the Chorus (Coda) and the ringing double stops just four bars later cleverly set against staccato F5 chord stabs.

# "FOR WHAT IT'S WORTH"
## *Buffalo Springfield*

Written by Stephen Stills in response to the "Sunset Strip riots" of 1966, "For What It's Worth" soon evolved into a protest song for all the calamities and social injustices surrounding the late 1960s. Featuring Stills on acoustic guitar, Neil Young on electric, and Richie Furay on 12-string acoustic, this classic perfectly encapsulates the less-is-more approach to songwriting.

## TONE

The 6- and 12-string acoustic guitars were either dreadnought- or jumbo-sized, likely a Martin D-28 6-string and a Gibson J-200 12-string. Similarly, you'll want to use a strum-friendly dreadnought-sized (or jumbo) acoustic to play these parts; either a 6- or a 12-string is perfectly acceptable.

As for the electric parts, Young typically played a 1961 Gretsch White Falcon during his Buffalo Springfield tenure. Although he normally plugged into his trusty 1959 Fender Deluxe, he would employ a tweed Fender Tremolux on this date, for that signature tremolo effect. The distortion you hear is natural amp breakup, and there's a healthy dose of reverb added in post-production. Likewise, you'll want to generate similar natural distortion if possible; otherwise, an overdrive or one of the popular "tweed" pedals should suffice. For the tremolo effect, set your rate around 3–4 with the intensity around 7, and use plenty of reverb.

## TECHNIQUE

If you're playing this song on your own, you'll want to stick to acoustic guitars. You could recreate the first four bars by simultaneously plucking the open low E string and the 12th-fret harmonic on the high E string for bars 1 and 3, and doing the same with the open A string, the 7th-fret harmonic on the high E for bars 2 and 4. Then, when it's time to strum, play an Asus2 chord instead of A major to include the B note otherwise sounded by the harmonic. This is an approach guitarist Richie Furay has used when performing the song solo in recent years.

If you're playing the electric part in a two-guitar band, Young's parts are fairly simple in terms of techniques. Note how he seamlessly moves between E major and E minor pentatonic/blues phrases in several positions across the neck—a priceless improvisational tool.

# "FORTUNATE SON"
## Creedence Clearwater Revival

Unlike Buffalo Springfield's "For What It's Worth" (see page 8), CCR's "Fortunate Son" actually was written as a protest song. Inspired by the lavish wedding of President Eisenhower's grandson to then-President Nixon's daughter, John Fogerty wrote the tune as vilification of the rich who plan wars and then enlist the poor to fight in them, knowing their own "fortunate sons" would never shed blood.

## TONE

Breaking with most classic rockers of the era, Fogerty used a *solid-state* 1968 Kustom K-200A-4 amp that featured built-in effects and a cabinet housing two 15" JBL speakers. The other key part of Fogerty's sound is his Gibson Les Paul Custom Black Beauty tuned down a whole step (D–G–C–F–A–D). The low tuning goes a long way in generating Fogerty's signature "swamp" tone, and if you really want to nail his tone, you'll need to tune down as well. Be aware, though, that if you use light-gauge strings (.009s or .010s), they won't sound as crisp when tuned down.

To get the tone, use a guitar, preferably Les Paul–style, equipped with a humbucker or even a P-90 in the bridge position. You'll also want to dial in a tone that's just breaking up on your amp, or engage a slight overdrive, and use your volume knob to clean it up for the opening riff.

## TECHNIQUE

The opening riff to "Fortunate Son" is a classic, comprising 6ths intervals that mirror the A–G–D–A chord progression. For the first two (A and G) dyads, use your middle finger on the 3rd string and your index finger on the 1st string. For the ensuing D and A dyads, you'll again use your middle finger on the 3rd string and, for the D, your ring finger on the 1st string. Though we typically recommend hybrid picking for 6ths licks like this, it sounds like Fogerty's picking those high notes, and so should you!

In the Interlude, if you're the lone guitarist, follow the Gtr. 2 part. Striking the low A note in concert with the dyads is optional, but if you do, you might want to use hybrid picking (fingers pluck the dyads while your pick strikes the open A). Either way, be sure to maintain that low A pedal between the chords.


# "GO YOUR OWN WAY"
## Fleetwood Mac

Few bands have have undergone as radically a change in style as Fleetwood Mac. Born as a British blues band led by the criminally underrated Peter Green on guitar, the group in the early 1970s transformed to a pop-leaning rock group led by the also-criminally underrated Lindsey Buckingham on guitar. "Go Your Own Way" is just one of at least eight tracks from the brilliant *Rumours* album that to this day *still* sees regular rotation on rock and AC radio.

## TONE

Although Buckingham is widely recognized as the #1 endorsee of Rick Turner guitars, *Rumours* was recorded prior to that. According to Turner, Buckingham used a Fender Strat outfitted with an Alembic Stratoblaster cranked to full 12dB boost, played through Hiwatt amps (which kept blowing up as a result of the Stratoblaster) for much of the *Rumours* album. When he first joined Fleetwood Mac, Buckingham also used an old Sony 2-track tape machine as an overdrive unit! More recently, his setup has been the Rick Turner Model 1 through a Boss OD-1 and into a Mesa/Boogie Tremoverb. Similarly, you can nail the "Go Your Own Way" tone using a Strat or single-coil guitar into an overdrive pedal to the front of a clean tube amp, and if you're going to try to cop the feedback notes, you might want a boost pedal in line as well.

## TECHNIQUE

The main guitar part to follow is Gtr. 2, though if you have a second guitarist in your band, you'll want to complement that part with the acoustic guitar capoed at the 5th fret—an often forgotten yet integral part of Buckingham's brilliant orchestration.

The other key element in this song is paying close attention to Buckingham's use of the slight palm mute in concert with striking various portions of the barre chords. It's subtle yet so important. If you play it with a consistent palm mute hitting only the power chords, you'll sound stiff and stale. Listen closely to how Buckingham loosens the mute and to how he intermingles power chords with full-on triad voicings.

# "HAD TO CRY TODAY"
*Blind Faith*

One of rock's earliest "supergroups," Blind Faith featured Cream vets Eric Clapton and Ginger Baker as well as Traffic's Steve Winwood and Family's Ric Grech. Their 1969 self-titled album—the band's first and only release—spawned two hits ("Can't Find My Way Home" and "In the Presence of the Lord") at the time, plus the now classic guitar riff-rocker "Had to Cry Today," penned by Winwood.

## TONE

Fresh out of Cream, in which he made famous the "woman tone," Clapton picked up a mid-1960s reverse Gibson Firebird with mini-humbuckers for the Blind Faith sessions and used a Fender Tele outfitted with a Stratocaster neck live. He plugged into Fender Dual Showman and Marshall amps. If you've got an axe with mini-humbuckers, great; otherwise, given the choice between humbuckers and single-coils, go with the humbuckers (bridge position). Coax some overdrive from the distortion channel on your amp or use an overdrive pedal with a generous amount of gain.

## TECHNIQUE

There is a *lot* of guitar playing happening here, most of it based in various minor pentatonic scales. If you're playing this with another guitarist, you'll just divide the parts as written. If you're doing this one alone, you should primarily follow the Gtr. 1 part, to account for all those terrific lead fills and 10ths intervals, but you may occasionally want to toss in the background arpeggios instead. Clapton's solo, if not as aggressive and epic as his take in "Crossroads," certainly draws from the same well of licks. Be sure to hit the bends at pitch, especially the 1-1/2-step over-bends and the ones with his sweet vibrato added on top.

The studio panning effect heard at the start of the outro solos can't really be duplicated live, but a reverse delay or reverse reverb can provide the desired performance effect.

# "KEEP YOUR HANDS TO YOURSELF"
*Georgia Satellites*

Just as new wave and hair metal were taking over the airwaves, a little ol' roots-rock outfit called the Georgia Satellites, led by singer/guitarist Dan Baird along with lead guitarist Rick Richards, blasted onto the scene. The band's hit single "Keep Your Hands to Yourself," along with its cheeky music video, introduced the Southern rock sound to the MTV generation.

## TONE

This quintessential rootsy blues rocker features the quintessential rootsy blues-rock tone. In this case, it comes courtesy of Baird's 1957 Fender Esquire and Richards's Dan Armstrong plexi guitar. Given the pair's affinity for vintage gear, it's quite likely Baird played the riff through a vintage tweed amp, with Richards going more of a Marshall route for the fatter-sounding fills.

Likewise, you'll want to use a Tele, Esquire, or other similarly single-coil–equipped guitar through an overdriven tube amp. For the solo and fills, you can kick in an overdrive such as a Tube Screamer or even a boost pedal to fatten the sound.

## TECHNIQUE

The main riff and rhythm part is about as basic and straightforward as it gets, so let's take a look at the 4-bar Interlude. This double stop–driven part contains three instances of double-stop bends at the 7th fret. I prefer to barre my ring finger across both strings and perform the bend; however, if you're having trouble with that approach, you might want to try fretting each string individually—either with your middle and ring fingers or your ring and pinky fingers, on strings 2 and 1, respectively, and then executing the bends. Same applies for the outro solo, particularly for the held double-stop bend in bar 6; however, when you reach bars 23–26, you may find the barre technique more conducive to the feel.

# "LIFE IN THE FAST LANE"
*Eagles*

When talk turns to guitar heroes, Eagles guitarists Joe Walsh and Don Felder are *rarely* mentioned, yet their solo on "Hotel California" is arguably one of the top 5 guitar solos ever put to tape. On that same album resides another all-time great rock guitar riff—"Life in the Fast Lane"—which Joe Walsh originally wrote as a warm-up exercise. Here's what you need to know.

## TONE

Walsh recorded the song's main riff using a 1950s Fender Strat, whereas Don Felder used his 1959 Gibson Les Paul. Both played through overdriven Fender Tweed Deluxe amps. Overall, the tone is quite raw, with no effects until the tape flange that was added to the Interlude in post-production.

The overriding sound in this song is that honky Fender Strat, so you'll want to use a similar single-coil guitar, engaging the bridge pickup. Since attaining natural tube overdrive on a tweed amp is a rather loud affair, use an overdrive pedal with the gain or drive control up fairly high to get the tone, with plenty of mids and highs. Although you technically need a thru-zero flanger (a rather pricy toy) in that famous Interlude, you can approximate the effect with a standard flanger pedal by setting the rate quite low with the frequency and depth about halfway.

## TECHNIQUE

The main riff is a pretty straightforward E minor pentatonic affair, except the rhythmic displacement that occurs at every fourth iteration—be sure to start on the "and" of beat 4 for that last one. After the main riff, the song is littered with cool licks and fills ranging from single-note lines to 6ths intervals and long, slow double-stop bends. For the double-stop bends in bar 10 of intro and bar 5 of the final verse, you'll need to barre both the 2nd and 3rd strings with one finger and pull the string downward (toward the floor) to generate the indicated bends of a full step on the 3rd string and a half step on the 2nd string. If you push up, the bend displacements will be reversed.

# "LIGHTS"
## *Journey*

Arguably the king of the melodic guitar solo, Journey's Neal Schon drew much of his early influence from soul and R&B singers like Aretha Franklin and Donny Hathaway, working to mimic their vocal phrasing on guitar. "Lights," from Journey's 1980 album *Infinity*, is a prime example of those R&B roots.

## TONE

Throughout his career, Schon has largely been a devotee of the Gibson Les Paul, with detours down the paths of his own Schon guitars and, recently, PRS. "Lights," however, was recorded with a 1963 Fender Strat (neck pickup) through a Marshall plexi. The Strat tone is so integral to this tune that Schon brings one on tour just for this tune, so you'll want to use one as well, if possible. As for amps, try a tube amp with its power-tube section being pushed hard, to get that breakup tone. You can then add a touch of fuzz or overdrive for that extra bit of hair—especially for the solo.

## TECHNIQUE

I hope your fret hand's pinky finger is in good shape, because you're going to use it—*a lot*. Throughout the tune, Schon employs all sorts of suspensions and embellishments, mostly with his pinky, to create a deeply R&B-inspired 6/8 groove. In fact, in the entire 8-bar intro, the only embellishment *not* performed with your pinky is the suspended 4th (D) on the A chord in bar 4.

The solo is set almost exclusively in D major pentatonic (D–E–F♯–A–B), moving between 10th and 7th positions. The trickiest section is also one of the solo's signature sections—the descending 4ths. When attacking these 4ths intervals, which occur on adjacent string pairs, you'll want to use "outside" alternate picking. In other words, pick the note on the higher string using an upstroke followed by a downstroke on the lower string.

# "MESSAGE IN A BOTTLE"
## *The Police*

Guitarist Andy Summers has called "Message in a Bottle" his favorite Police track, and it is widely regarded not only as the song that cemented a superstar career for the trio but also as one of the greatest guitar riffs of all time. Ironically, though, it was a *bassist*—Sting—who wrote this "stacked 5ths" masterpiece.

## TONE

Summers has used a lot of guitars in his career, but his 1963 (some say 1961) Fender Telecaster with a Gibson PAF humbucker in the neck and a built-in preamp is undoubtedly his "go-to" axe. Although Summers's legendary clean tones came through a pair of modded Marshall plexis (!) in live settings, he reportedly used either a Fender Twin or a Fender Princeton in the studio during that era.

A Tele or Strat-style guitar through a clean tube amp will get you started, but it's the modulation that's key to copping the Summers sound. Contrary to popular belief, that is not a chorus effect you hear on "Message in a Bottle." Instead, it's a recipe consisting of a flanger (Electro-Harmonix Electric Mistress) set for just a bit of swirl (slow rate, not much depth), a slight echo (Echoplex) to fatten the sound, a bit of compression (MXR Dynacomp),and just the slightest hint of overdrive. You *can* use a chorus pedal to approximate the tone, but a flanger is necessary to nail it.

## TECHNIQUE

For the main riff, which comprises a progression of sus2 chords formed by stacked 5ths, Summers uses his fret hand's index, *middle*, and pinky fingers on strings 6, 5, and 4, respectively, throughout. You can do the same, though most guitarists typically prefer to use their ring finger on string 5. You should also note that Gtr. 1 represents the main riff, whereas Gtr. 2 is the harmonized complement. Thus, if you're playing the song as a lone guitarist, play the Gtr. 1 part. The other standout part in terms of technique is Summers's harp harmonics in the final two bars of the chorus. To execute this part, form a barre across all six strings at the 2nd fret. Then, holding the pick between your thumb and middle finger, lightly touch the 6th string *directly above* the 14th fret while simultaneously picking the string. Next, use your pick hand's ring finger to pluck the 3rd string. Continue the pattern moving up one string each time, alternating harmonics and fretted notes. Once you have the hang of it, you'll find it's actually not as challenging as it sounds.


# "PEACE OF MIND"
## *Boston*

What can you say about Boston's self-titled debut album that hasn't been said before? To this day, *every one* of the disc's eight tracks get regular radio airplay—an achievement that not even Michael Jackson or the Beatles can boast. "Peace of Mind" is the second track on the album and arguably the band's second-most popular song, after "More Than a Feeling."

## TONE

Guitarist Tom Scholz, who holds a Master's degree in engineering from M.I.T., used his knowledge and love of tinkering to design his own amps and effects (the Rockman), in the process creating one of the most unique guitar sounds in rock history. But … the Rockman line came *after* the first album. So what did he use here?

Scholz's main axe is a Gibson Les Paul goldtop with P-90 soapbar pickups. A similarly equipped axe, or one with humbuckers, will do the trick for you (use the bridge pickup throughout). He played through a dimed Marshall with a Power Soak attenuator. You can achieve similar results without blowing your eardrums using a rich distortion pedal or a high-gain master volume amp (but don't wade into heavy metal gain levels). Roll off the lows and boost the mids (around 800 Hz to 1KHz). You'll also want to add a touch of chorus and lots of compression.

## TECHNIQUE

After the iconic acoustic strum opener (which should be strummed with authority on a dreadnought), the main lead riff comes in, with the first 12 notes all played along the 5th string. Sure, this is rather inefficient, and most guitarists just play it all in 4th position (you can, too), but video evidence shows this is how Mr. Scholz plays it, so that's how we present it! Truthfully, playing it as written in combination with Scholz's massive guitar sound indeed makes the riff sound even more epic. In the solo, note Scholz's brilliant deployment of motifs. In terms of technique, the licks are pretty straightforward but occasionally require quick position shifts, so if you're not comfortable with those moves, focus specifically on those transition points until they're smooth.


# "REELING IN THE YEARS"
## *Steely Dan*

Steely Dan has produced some of the most technically brilliant music the rock and pop world has ever heard, and "Reeling in the Years" is, at least commercially, their crowning achievement. Guitarist Elliott Randall played the iconic solo here, which Jimmy Page has called his "favorite guitar solo of all time."

## TONE

Randall has reportedly said that he recorded the solo on his 1963 Fender Stratocaster, using a neck-position humbucker, played through an Ampeg SVT bass amp turned all the way up. Was he pulling someone's leg? Who knows, but it's nonetheless one of the all-time classic guitar tones. To match the tone on the guitar solo and fills, plug a Strat-style guitar into a clean tube amp, with a fuzz box inline set for a good amount of "hair." For the famous Interlude sections, substitute a slight overdrive for the fuzz.

## TECHNIQUE

There are so many elements here that come together to make this a classic track. One of them is Randall's tasty use of fills during the choruses. While many are straightforward, the triplet driven descending line of 4ths and 3rds in bars 15–16 is a tricky endeavor. Because the phrase is arranged in two-note pairs and using hammer-ons, it's easy to fall into the trap of playing it in an eighth-note fashion, rather than the indicated triplet rhythm. First get the pattern, including the required position shifts, under your fingers. Then focus on nailing the triplet rhythm.

Randall has said that the solo "just came to [him]," and both the main and outro solos most certainly have an improvised feel. Be sure to nail all of the "essential" phrases, but for some parts, like the chromaticism in bars 5–8 of the main solo or the legato-fest in bars 7–8 of the outro, just let loose and go with the flow.

## "REFUGEE"
*Tom Petty*

When asked what was the favorite song he'd ever written, guitarist Mike Campbell of Tom Petty and the Heartbreakers said, "'Refugee' always makes me happy … It always sounds like it really captured a moment." The lead track from Petty's 1979 breakout album *Damn the Torpedoes*, "Refugee" helped establish the band as one of the top rock acts of the era, and as time has shown, of all time.

### TONE

Campbell wrote "Refugee" on his late 1960s Gibson Les Paul goldtop. However, when it came time to record the track, Campbell says it took over 100 takes over a couple of months using every amp he could find before they got the final track. Frustrated, he came into the studio one day and found a Marshall that someone had brought in. He plugged a Tele into it, and that's the sound you hear on the record. So your obvious choice is a Tele into a Marshall, but a Strat-style or a P90-equipped Les Paul style guitar through a Marshall or tweed tube amp pushed to distortion will get you there. Try rolling some high end off your signal using the guitar's tone knob. If you can't play that loud, place an overdrive pedal inline.

### TECHNIQUE

"Refugee" features Mike Campbell's efficient and tasteful guitar technique at its best. The song is in F♯ minor, and as such, Campbell deftly mines the F♯ minor pentatonic scale with golden results. Note the final beat of the signature intro guitar solo: striking the 2nd-fret F♯ on string 1 then sliding up to the 7th-fret F♯ on string 2—a nod to T-Bone Walker and B.B. King. Similarly, Campbell's use of double stops reflects the influence of Chuck Berry.

In both the Organ/Guitar Solo and the Outro, use your ring finger for the slides along the 2nd string played against the open E string. It's easy to arch that finger thus allowing the open E to ring freely *and* it sets up perfectly for the 14th-position licks that follow.

## "ROCK AND ROLL NEVER FORGETS"
*Bob Seger*

Though Bob Seger had already formed and found tremendous success with his Silver Bullet Band, he frequently used the Muscle Shoals studio musicians for his sessions, including on *Night Moves*, which is arguably Seger's greatest studio album and a highlight of late-'70s rock 'n' roll. However, it is the SBB, featuring guitarist Drew Abbott, heard on "Rock and Roll Never Forgets."

### TONE

Abbott's main axe through the years has been a 1968 Gibson Les Paul goldtop, though he also frequently used Gibson Explorers live. But in an interview with ChopShop Radio, Abbott said he used his 1962 Fender Strat on a lot of the early Seger material. He also used a vintage tweed Fender Bassman 4x10. To recreate the tone, you can use either a Strat in the bridge position but with some top end rolled off or a P-90–equipped guitar straight into a distorted tweed amp—no effects.

### TECHNIQUE

In that same interview with ChopShop Radio, Abbott described his solo in "Rock and Roll Never Forgets" as "almost country—kind of major-based." Sure enough, using pedal steel–style oblique bends, 6ths licks, and major pentatonic scales, Abbott fires off a tasty little country-style solo in the midst of a song about rock 'n' roll—but it sticks like sausage gravy on biscuits! For the opening oblique bend in the solo, barre your pinky across strings 2–1 at the 14th fret. For the ensuing 6ths licks in E, use your middle finger on string 3 and your ring finger on string 1. Finally, you'll need to make a quick position shift between the down- and upbeat of beat 4 in bar 6. Same advice applies to the similar licks found in the Outro. Make note, however, of Abbott's seamless alternation of E major and minor pentatonic soloing.

# "ROUNDABOUT"

*Yes*

When discussion of the all-time great guitar technicians ensues, names like Eddie Van Halen, Randy Rhoads, Joe Satriani, and John Petrucci typically (and justly) are spewed as icons. But Yes guitarist Steve Howe—whose monster chops are informed as much by classical guitar and Chet Atkins as they are by rock 'n' roll—predates them all! His playing on "Roundabout," from Yes's great *Fragile* album, clearly shows Howe as one of those all-time greats.

## TONE

Though he's best known as the rock 'n' roll torchbearer for the Gibson ES-175, Howe used his 1959 Gibson ES5 Switchmaster for the electric parts on most of *Fragile*, including "Roundabout." This is plugged into a Fender Dual Showman head fed through a 2x15 cab. The slight distortion he gets comes courtesy of an old Marshall fuzz box. To get this sound, use a semi-hollowbody guitar such as a Gibson ES-335, plugged into a very clean amp with your preferred fuzz pedal in between.

The famous Intro is played on a nylon-string acoustic, but the Verse riff is played on steel-string acoustics. If you've got to choose one, go with the steel-string acoustic—just be sure to use the fleshy portion of your fingertips to play the Intro, for a slightly muted tone similar to that of a nylon-string.

## TECHNIQUE

Besides the requisite classical technique in the Intro, the first challenging part is the natural harmonic Verse riff. Play the harmonics over the 12th fret with your ring finger, then shift down the neck to play the 7th-fret harmonics with your ring finger and the 5th-fret harmonics with your index finger.

The fingerings that Howe uses during his Guitar Solo later in the tune are fairly straightforward, but they are deceptively fast! For best results, use a metronome to practice these primarily 16th-note based lines cleanly, gradually increasing the tempo until you can match Howe's blazing fingers. As a sole guitar player, stick with the Gtr. 7 part.

# "TOM SAWYER"

*Rush*

Despite the success of 1980's *Permanent Waves* and its hit single "The Spirit of Radio," it was 1981's *Moving Pictures* and lead track "Tom Sawyer" that turned Rush into a staple of rock radio and put them on the path to becoming the greatest progressive rock band in history.

## TONE

Guitarist Alex Lifeson—a longtime Les Paul and ES-355 devotee—tracked "Tom Sawyer" using a Gibson Howard Roberts Fusion model. For amplification, Lifeson used Hiwatts and Marshall 4140 combos, which are relatively clean amps. He used a MXR distortion pedal, thickening the stew with a BOSS CE-1 chorus unit and Roland delays. You'll want to use a guitar equipped with a bridge-position humbucker, played through either a distortion pedal or the distorted channel of your amp with generous amount of gain. Place a chorus pedal (low mix, just enough to fatten the sound and add a slight swirl) and a slight delay in the chain as well.

## TECHNIQUE

The main riff comprising power chord and sus chords needs no explanation, but the bass line–driven Verse riff pedaled against the sometimes unison B notes (open 2nd string and 4th fret of 3rd string) presents a small challenge. If you watch Lifeson play this part, you'll notice that his fret hand fingers are quite arched, and that 4th-fret B note (3rd string) is fretted with his pinky finger, which increases the range of motion of his index and middle fingers to play the underlying bass line. As you play this part, don't worry about whether you strike the fretted B, the open B, or even both.

Lifeson's solo in "Tom Sawyer" is "comped"; that is, the solo is pieced together taking the best parts of several takes. So when you work on this solo, don't worry so much about the minutiae as capturing the overall vibe. For example, when attacking the final two bars containing whole-step bends at the 19th fret, don't worry so much about the precise rhythm as making each one count.

# "UP ON CRIPPLE CREEK"

*The Band*

After serving as Bob Dylan's backing band, The Band released their first album, *The Big Pink*, in 1968. But it was their follow-up 1969 self-titled release that made Robbie Robertson, Levon Helm, and company genuine stars. "Up on Cripple Creek" has inspired many lyrical interpretations over the years, but with its swampy New Orleans groove yet light and catchy air the song has become a classic rock staple.

## TONE

Before we get to the guitars, if you're wondering what's generating that jaw harp sound in various parts, it's a Clavinet D6 through a Vox wah pedal. As for the guitar sound, Robertson played a Fender Telecaster for the first two Band albums. He also used a variety of Fender amps, possibly a tweed Bassman here. Similarly, using the bridge pickup on a standard Strat or Tele plugged into a clean tube amp with a fairly neutral EQ setting will get you there for this tune.

## TECHNIQUE

The sparse opening riff (Gtr. 1) augurs the 16th-note syncopation that runs throughout the song. If you're not comfortable counting 16th notes (*one–ee–and–uh, two–ee–and–uh*, etc.), take it slow and make sure you're hitting notes on the correct subdivisions. Bars 3–4 of the Verse (Gtr. 2) may appear at first glance to be challenging until you realize every attack is on the downbeat. But come the Chorus, the syncopation kicks it into high gear. Again, count out the rhythm slowly to make sure you're hitting the right subdivisions, but also listen to the track, to get a feel for the swampy roots-rock groove.

# "WILD NIGHT"

*John Mellencamp*

John Mellencamp is not only one of the greatest songwriters of the past 30 years but also has been blessed to work with some of the finest musicians on the planet during that time, including guitarists Mike Wanchic, Larry Crane, David Grissom, and Andy York. It's the brilliant fretwork of Wanchic and York that we hear on "Wild Night," a Van Morrison cover that Mellencamp along with bassist extraordinaire Meshell Ndegeocello turned into a smash hit in 1994.

## TONE

Andy York played the guitars on this track, with Mike Wanchic on lap steel. York is known to choose from a plethora of weapons, notably early PRS Customs and Fender Telecasters and Stratocasters, and various Gibson models. The tone here sounds like either a Tele or a Strat, using the bridge pickup, most likely plugged directly into a Fender tweed amp or possibly a Vox AC-30 top-boost. Note that clean and overdriven electric guitars are combined into a composite part here. To go it alone, use a slightly overdriven tone, preferably natural tube distortion from a tweed-style amp, and then use your guitar's volume knob to reach the right mix of clean and drive. For the solo and lead fills, turn your volume up all the way for max drive and bite.

For the slide parts, unless you have a lap steel, you'll want to tune an electric guitar to open G and have at it through an overdriven tweed amp.

## TECHNIQUE

The hook in this song is Ndegeocello's memorable bass riff, which is transcribed here for guitar. For the trills, it's easiest to use your index and middle fingers, even though that requires quick position shifts. Specifically, fret the low G with your index finger, the octave G with your ring finger, then shift up to 4th position to execute the trill, shift back down to 3rd position and repeat.

For the unison bends in the solo and later fills, make sure you bend that 15th-fret D note all the way to E and nail the pitch. To practice hitting the pitch consistently, first strike the 12th-fret E on the 1st string, then hit the D and bend until the pitch matches. Do this repeatedly, until you can bend in tune consistently.

from Robert Palmer - *Riptide*

# Addicted to Love

**Words and Music by Robert Palmer**

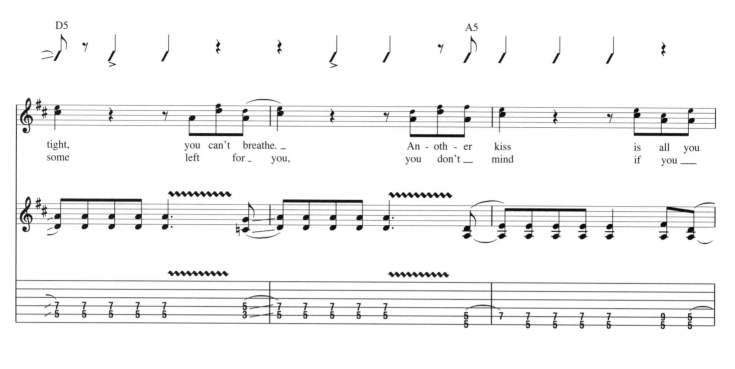

**Pre-Chorus**

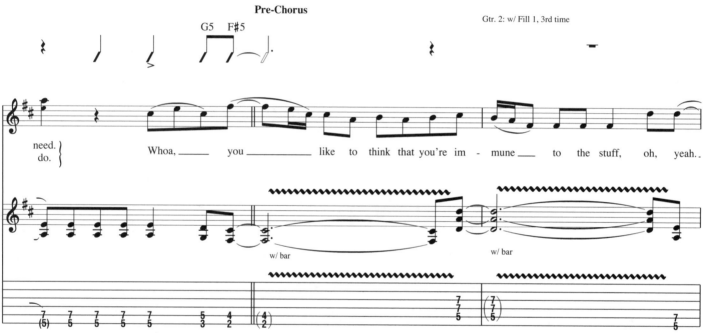

Gtr. 2: w/ Fill 1, 3rd time

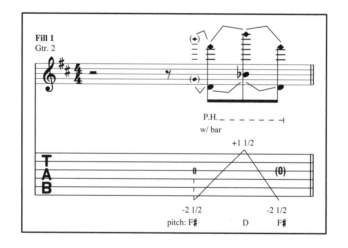

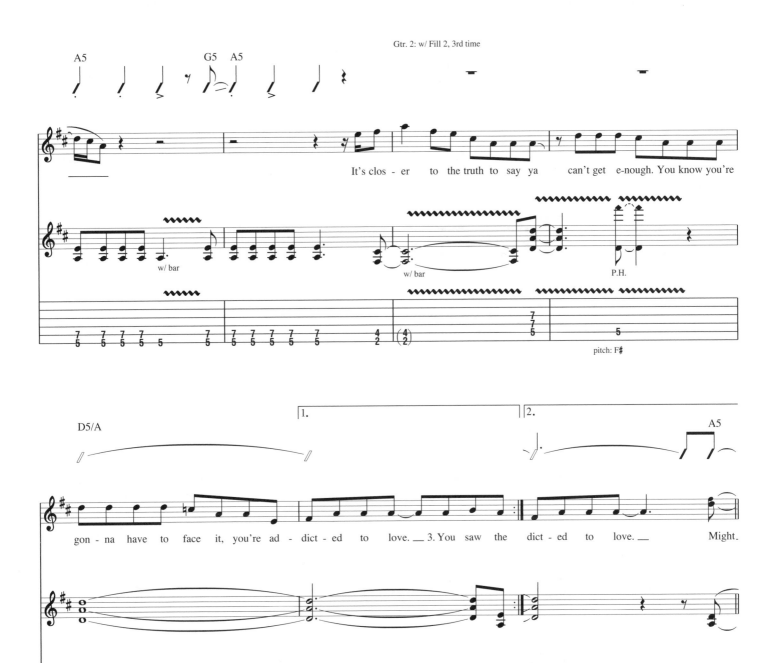

It's clos - er to the truth to say ya can't get e-nough. You know you're

gon - na have to face it, you're ad - dict - ed to love. __ 3. You saw the dict - ed to love. __ Might.

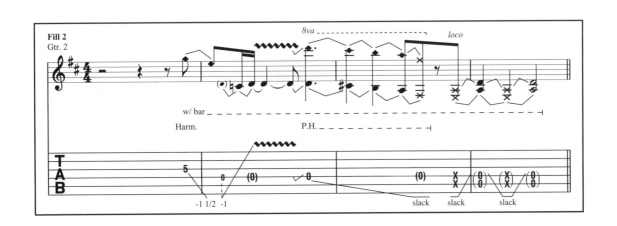

**Guitar Solo**

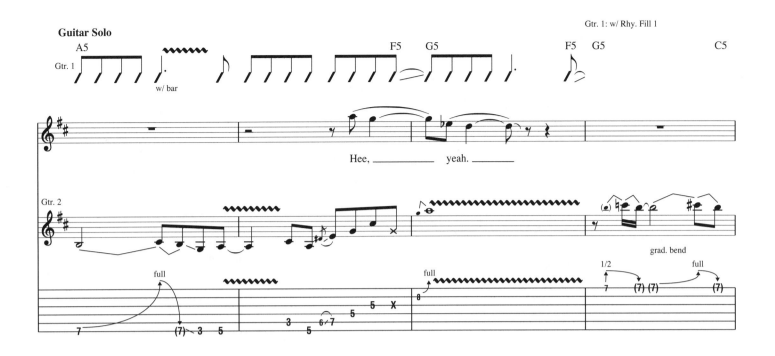

Hee, _____ yeah. _____

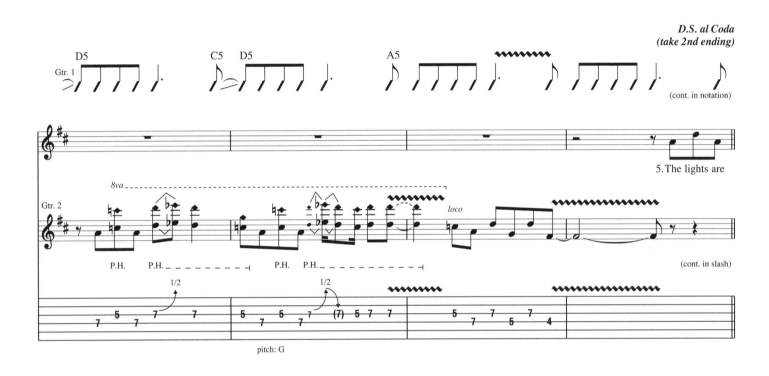

*D.S. al Coda*
*(take 2nd ending)*

(cont. in notation)

5. The lights are

(cont. in slash)

pitch: G

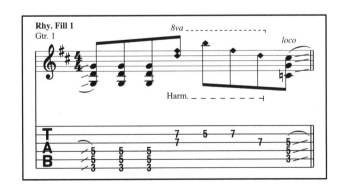

**Rhy. Fill 1**

## Coda

**Chorus**
*Begin Fade*

as well face it, you're ad - dict - ed to love. — Might — as well face it, you're ad -
(Oo, — yeah. _____ )

*Fade Out*

dict - ed to love. — Might — as well face it, you're ad - dict - ed to love. — Might — as well face it, you're ad -

*Additional Lyrics*

5. The lights are on, but you're not home.
   Your will is not your own.
   Your heart sweats, your teeth grind.
   Another kiss and you'll be mine.

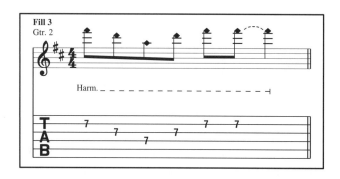

from Eric Clapton - *Eric Clapton*

# After Midnight

### Words and Music by J.J. Cale

(Gon - na shake your tam - bou - rine, ____ gon - na shake your tam - bou - rine. ____ )

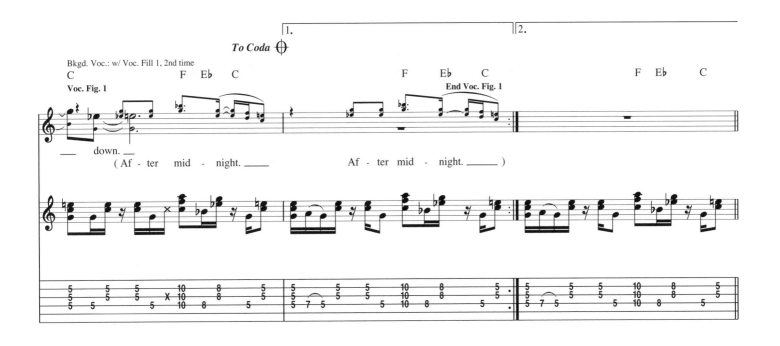

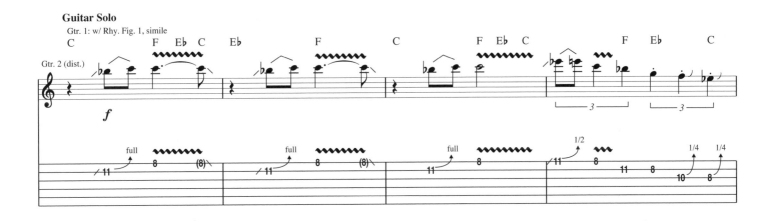

**Guitar Solo**

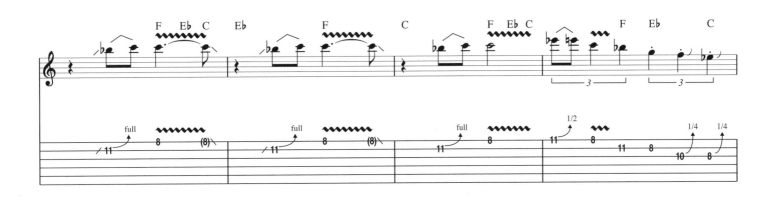

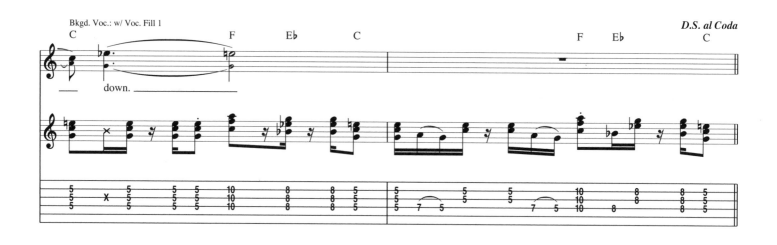

from Pink Floyd - *The Wall*

# Another Brick in the Wall, Part 2

**Words and Music by Roger Waters**

Gtr. 3: Drop D tuning:
(low to high) D-A-D-G-B-E

**\*\*Two gtrs. arr. for one.**

**\*\*\*2nd time, lead voc. doubled one octave higher by childrens' chorus.**

**†Set for one octave higher.**

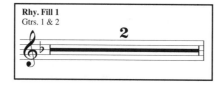

Gtrs. 1 & 2: w/ Rhy. Fig. 1 (2 times)

We don't need \_ no \_\_\_\_ thought con - trol. _____           No

Gtr. 3: w/ Riff A

dark sar - cas - m \_\_\_\_\_ in the class - room.

Teach - er, / Teach - ers,    leave \_\_\_ them \_\_\_\_ kids a - lone. \_\_\_

Gtrs. 1 & 2

Gtr. 3

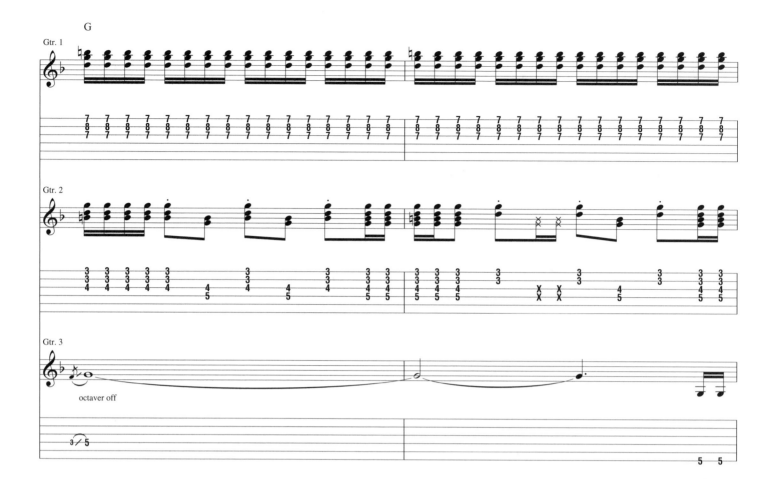

Hey,            teach-er,            leave {them/us} kids    a - lone.

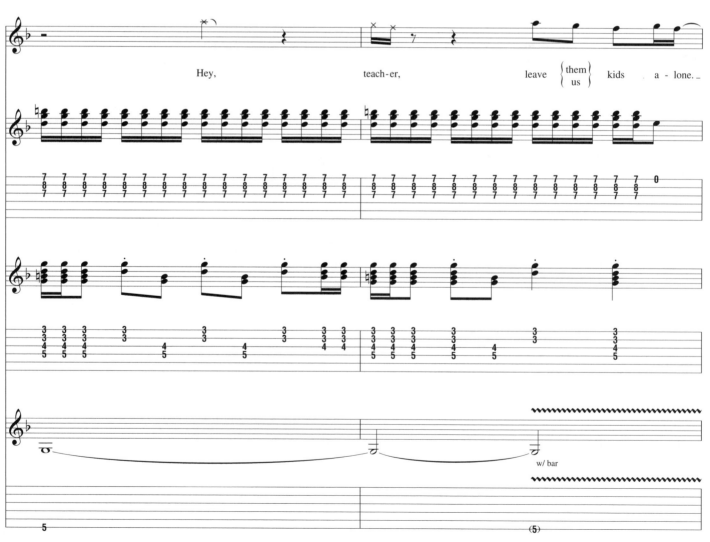

w/ bar

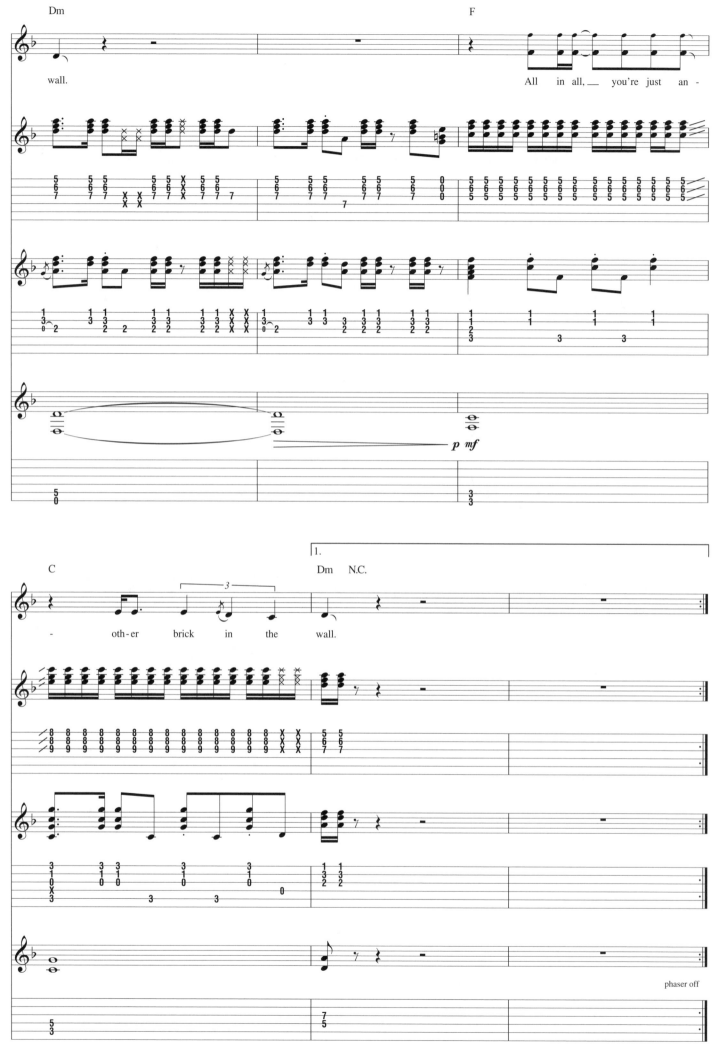

*Chord symbols reflect overall harmony.

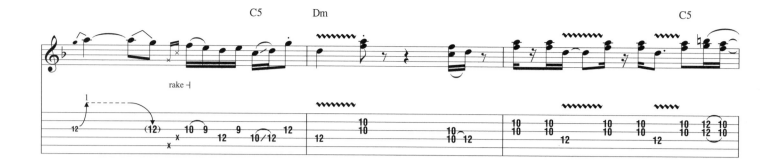

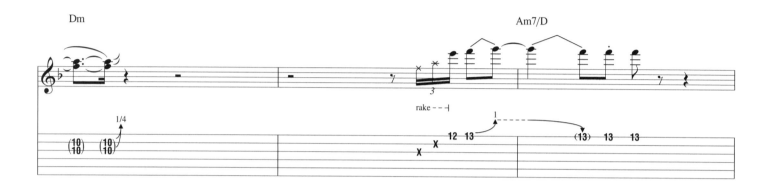

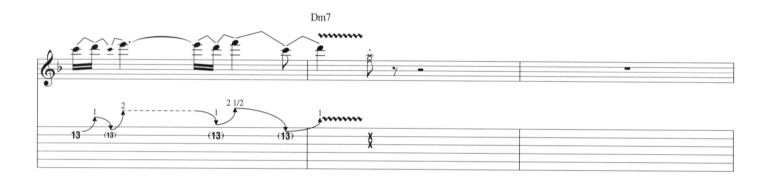

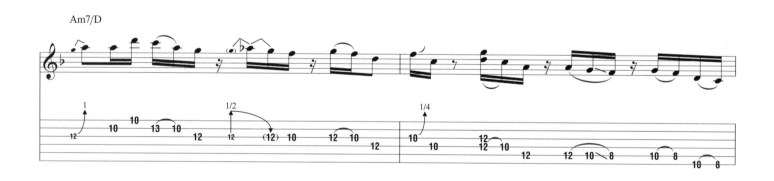

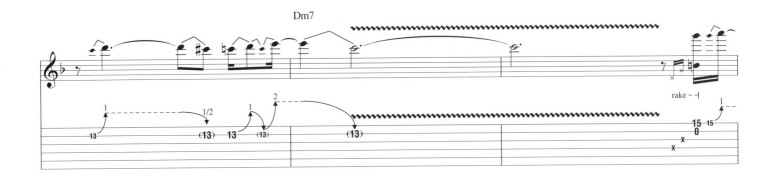

*Note on 2nd string sounds my bumping the string
when executing the vibrato on 1st string;
don't pick.

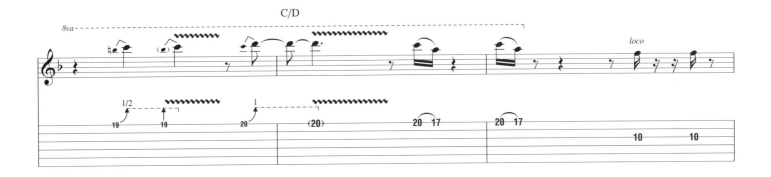

**Begin fade**

Gtr. 4 tacet

(Drums, misc. spoken voices & dial tone)

*Fade out*

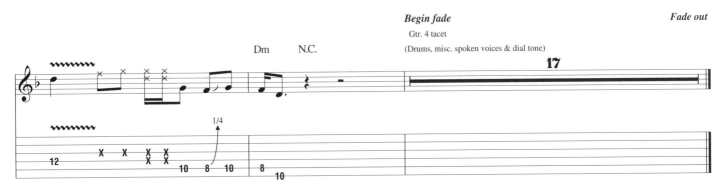

# Aqualung

**Words and Music by Ian Anderson and Jennie Anderson**

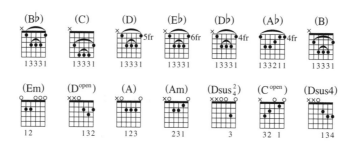

Gtrs. 2 & 4: Capo III

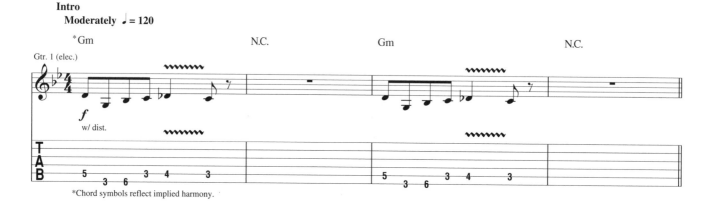

*Chord symbols reflect implied harmony.

**Symbols in parentheses represent chord names respective to capoed guitar and do not reflect actual sounding chords.
See top of page for chord diagrams pertaining to rhythm slashes.

*Symbols in parentheses represent chord names respective
to capoed guitar. Symbols above reflect actual sounding chords.

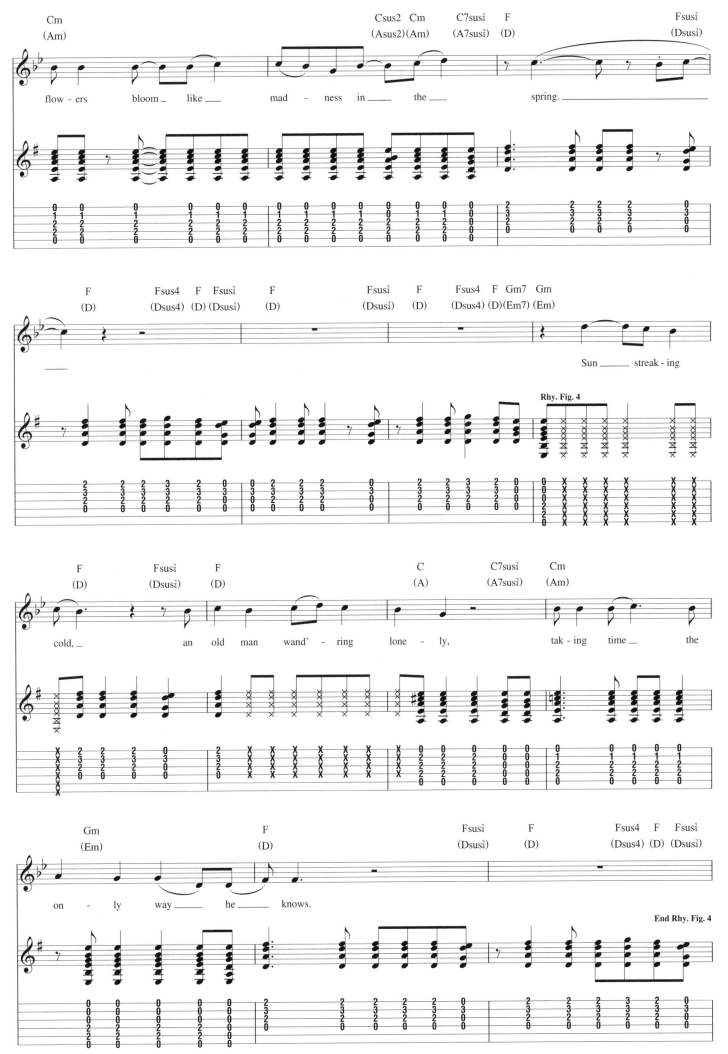

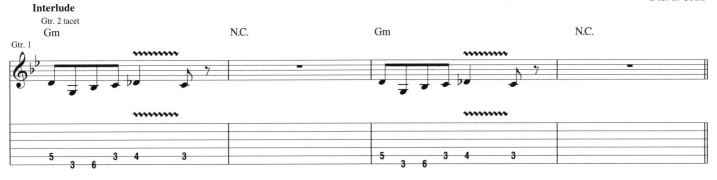

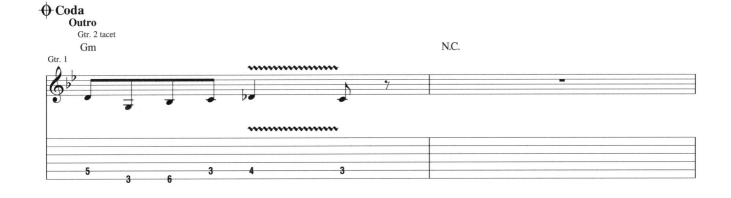

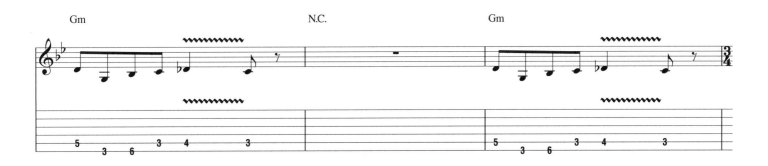

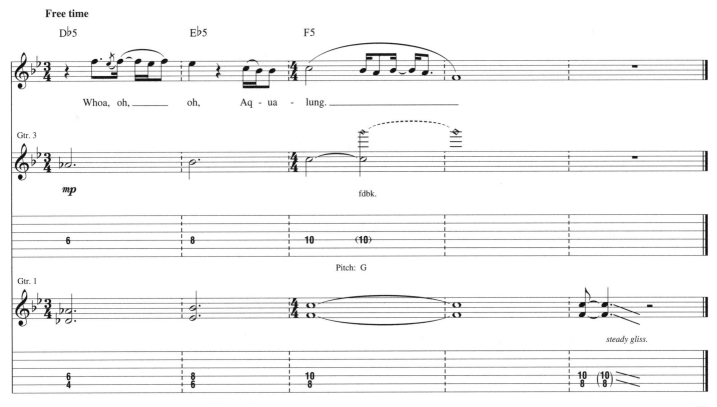

# Beat It

**Words and Music by Michael Jackson**

Tune down 1/2 step:
(low to high) E♭-A♭-D♭-G♭-B♭-E♭

**Intro**
**Moderately fast** ♩ = 140

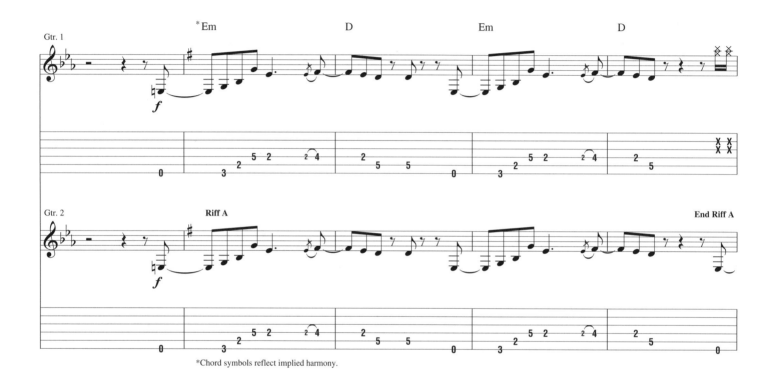

*Chord symbols reflect implied harmony.

**Verse**

Gtr. 2 tacet

1. They told him, "Don't you ev - er come a - round here. Don't wan - na see your face, you bet - ter
2. They're out to get you, bet - ter leave while you can, don't wan - na be a boy, you wan - na

Gtr. 1 **Rhy. Fig. 1**

dis - ap - pear." The fire's __ in their eyes, and their words are real - ly clear, so
be a man. You wan - na stay a - live, bet - ter do what you can, so

Gtr. 1: w/ Rhy. Fig. 1 (1st 7 meas.)

beat it. Just beat it. You bet - ter run; you bet - ter
beat it. Just beat it, oh! You have to show them that you're

**End Rhy. Fig. 1** **Riff B**

Gtr. 3 (clean)

*mf*

P.M. - - - - - - - - - - - - - - - - -

do what you can. Don't wan - na see no blood; don't be a ma - cho man. You
real - ly not scared, you're play - ing with your life, this ain't no truth or dare, oh! They'll

**End Riff B**

P.M. - - - - - - - - - - - - - - - - - - - - - - - - - - -

49

wan - na  be  tough,  bet - ter  do  what  you  can,  so  beat  it.  But  you
kick  you  then they beat you then they'll  tell  you  it's  fair,  so  beat  it.  But  you

𝄋 **Chorus**

Gtr. 3 tacet
3rd time, Gtr. 4: w/ Fill 1

wan - na  be  bad. } Just  beat  it,  beat  it.  No —
wan - na  be  bad. } (Beat  it,  beat  it.)

Gtrs. 1 & 2: w/ Riff A (last 2 meas.)

1st time, Gtrs. 1 & 2: w/ Riff A (2 times)
2nd & 3rd times, Gtrs. 1 & 2: w/ Riff A (3 times)

— one wants to be de - feat - ed,  show - in' how funk - y  strong —

— is  your  fight.  It  does - n't  mat - ter  who's — wrong  or  right.  Just

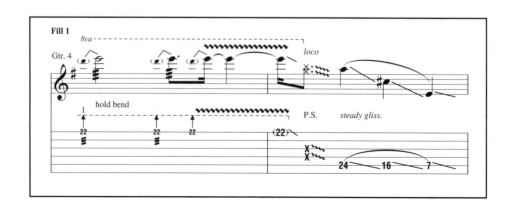

Fill 1

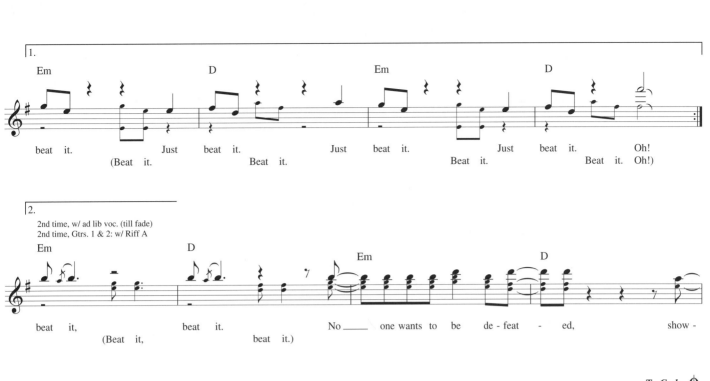

beat it. Just beat it. Just beat it. Just beat it. Oh!
(Beat it. Beat it. Beat it. Beat it. Oh!)

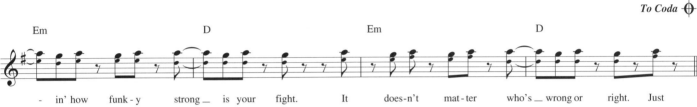

2nd time, w/ ad lib voc. (till fade)
2nd time, Gtrs. 1 & 2: w/ Riff A

beat it, beat it. No ___ one wants to be de - feat - ed, show -
(Beat it, beat it.)

*To Coda*

- in' how funk - y strong ___ is your fight. It does - n't mat - ter who's ___ wrong or right. Just

**Bridge**

beat it. Beat it.

Gtr. 2  **Riff C**                                    **End Riff C**

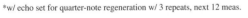
*w/ echo set for quarter-note regeneration w/ 3 repeats, next 12 meas.

Gtr. 2: w/ Riff C (2 3/4 times)

Beat it. Beat it.

Gtr. 1  **Riff D**                                    **End Riff D**

Gtr. 1: w/ Riff D (3 times)

Beat it.

**Guitar Solo**

Gtrs. 1 & 2: w/ Rhy. Fig. 1 (2 times)

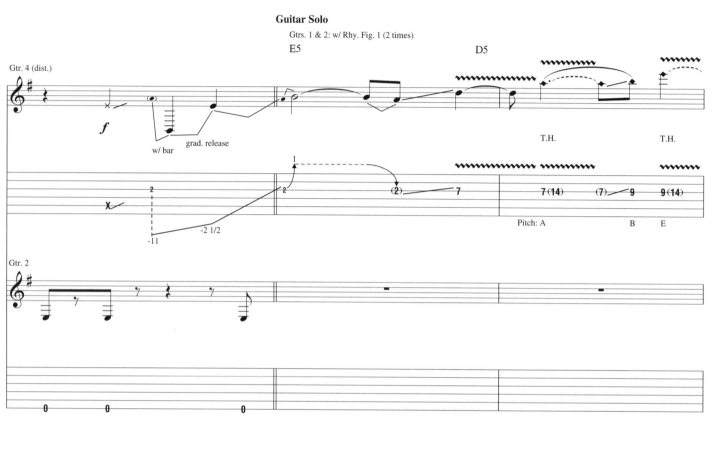

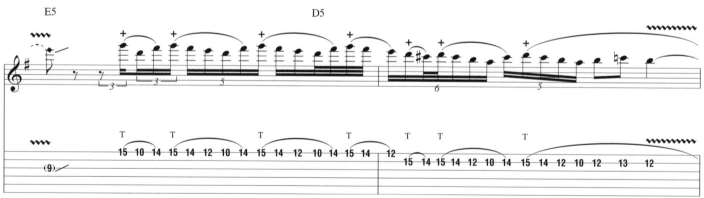

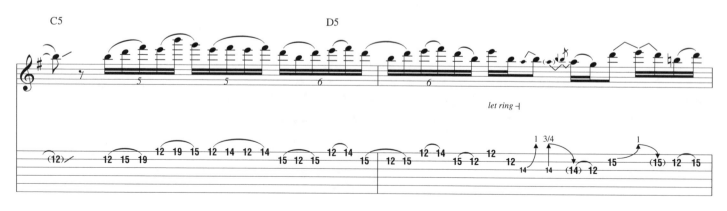

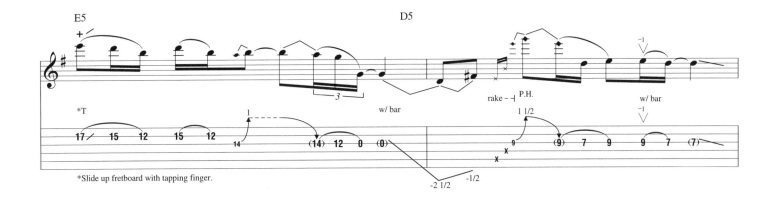

*Slide up fretboard with tapping finger.

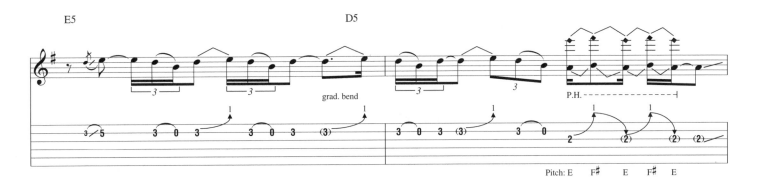

Pitch: E  F#  E  F#  E

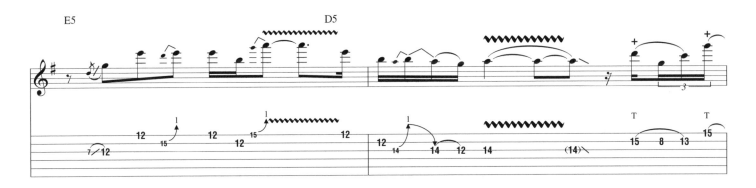

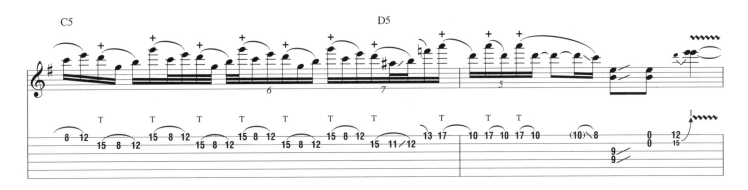

D.S. al Coda
(take 2nd ending)

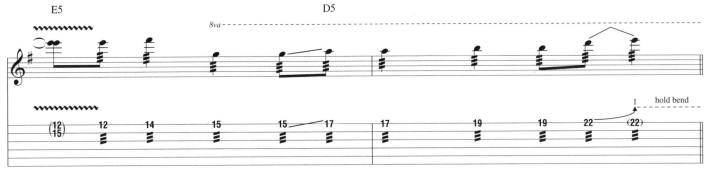

## ⊕ Coda

**Outro-Chorus**

beat it, beat it. No ___

(Beat it, beat it.)

*2nd time, Begin fade*

___ one wants to be de-feat - ed, show - in' how funk-y strong ___

___ is your fight. It does-n't mat-ter who's ___ wrong or right. Just

*Fade out*

Gtrs. 1 & 2: w/ Riff A (1st 3 meas.)

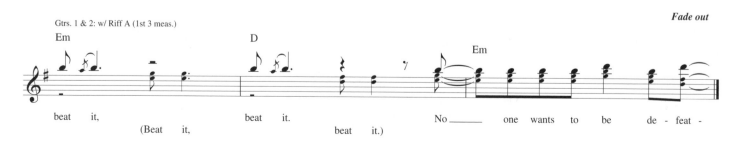

beat it, beat it. No ___ one wants to be de-feat -

(Beat it, beat it.)

54

from The Rolling Stones - *Sticky Fingers*

# Brown Sugar

### Words and Music by Mick Jagger and Keith Richards

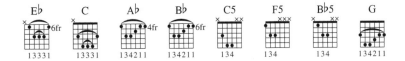

Gtr. 1: Open G tuning:
(low to high) D-G-D-G-B-D

**Intro**
**Moderately fast** ♩ = 128

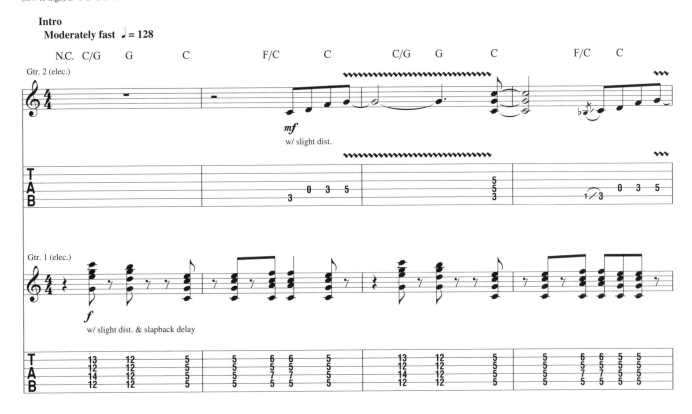

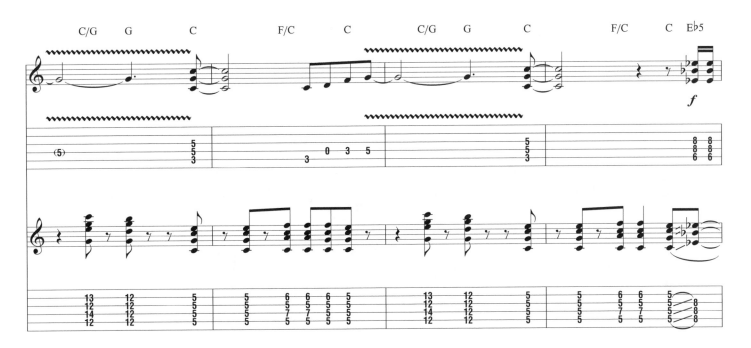

*See top of first page of song for chord diagrams pertaining to rhythm slashes.

1. Gold

let ring - - - - - - -

56

Gtrs. 2 & 3: w/ Rhy. Figs. 5 & 5A

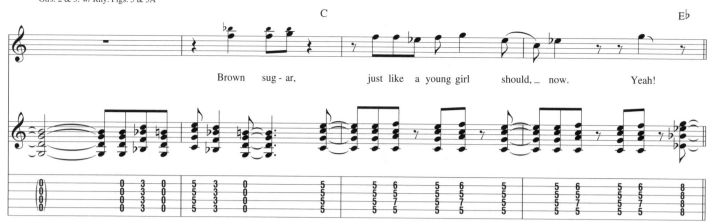

Brown sug-ar, just like a young girl should, _ now. Yeah!

**Sax Solo**

*Gtrs. 2 & 3: w/ Rhy. Figs. 1 & 1A (3 times)

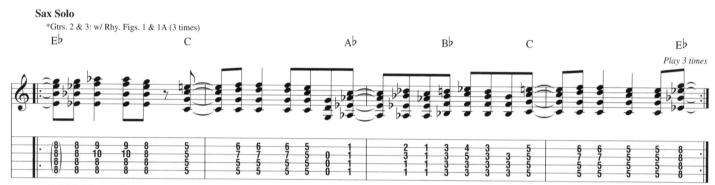

*2nd & 3rd times the first chord of Rhy. Fig. 1 is not struck but tied over from previous measure.

Ah, _____

good old _ brown sug-ar, how _ come you taste so good, babe? Ah, _____
(Brown sug-ar.)

**Chorus**

Gtr. 1: w/ Rhy. Fig. 6
Gtrs. 2 & 3: w/ Rhy. Figs. 4 & 4A

got me feel-in' now, you brown sug-ar, just like a black girl should, _ yeah. 3. Now, _____

**Verse**

Gtr. 3: w/ Rhy. Fig. 3A

_ I bet your ma-ma was a tent show queen, _ and ___ all her boy-friends were sweet six - teen, _ I'm _

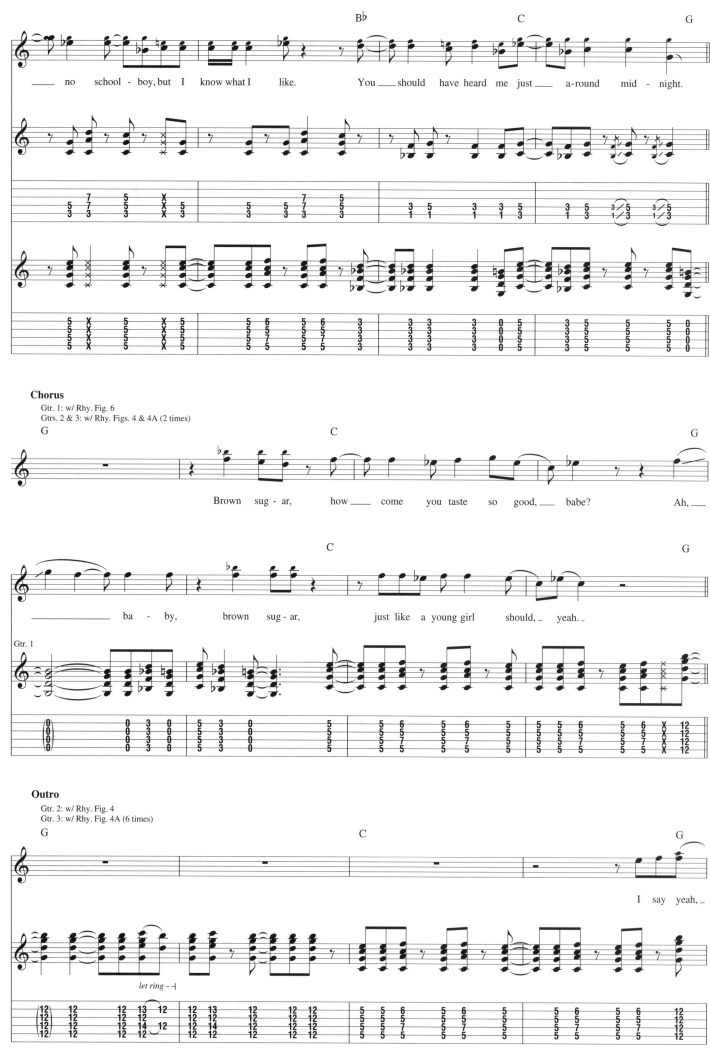

**Chorus**
Gtr. 1: w/ Rhy. Fig. 6
Gtrs. 2 & 3: w/ Rhy. Figs. 4 & 4A (2 times)

**Outro**
Gtr. 2: w/ Rhy. Fig. 4
Gtr. 3: w/ Rhy. Fig. 4A (6 times)

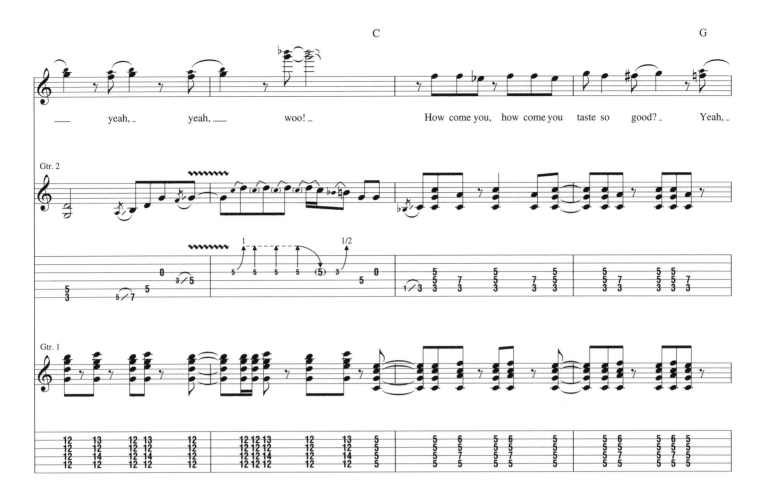

yeah, ___ yeah, ___ woo! ___   How come you, how come you taste so good? Yeah, ___

Gtr. 2

Gtr. 1

yeah, ___ yeah, ___ woo! ___   Just like a, just like a black girl should. Yeah, ___

Rhy. Fig. 7

End Rhy. Fig. 7

yeah,___   yeah,___   woo!___

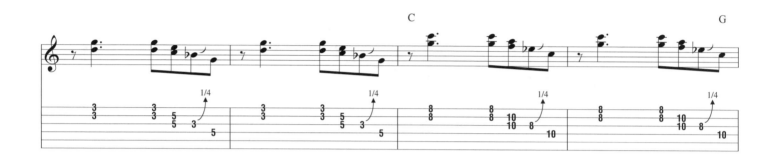

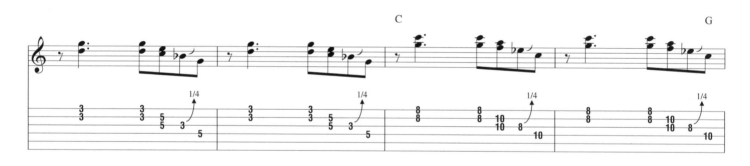

from The Doobie Brothers - *The Captain and Me*

# China Grove

**Words and Music by Tom Johnston**

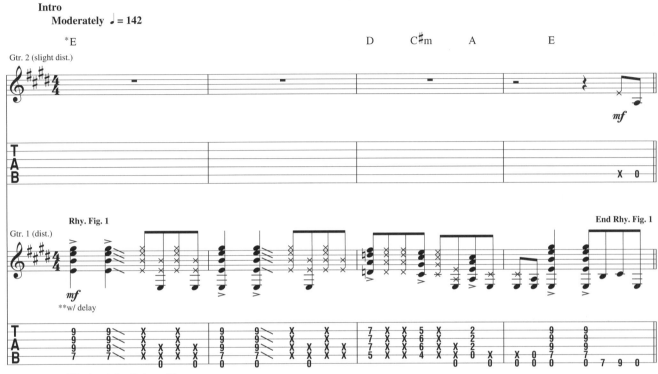

*Chord symbols reflect overall harmony.
**Set for quarter-note regeneration w/ 2 repeats.

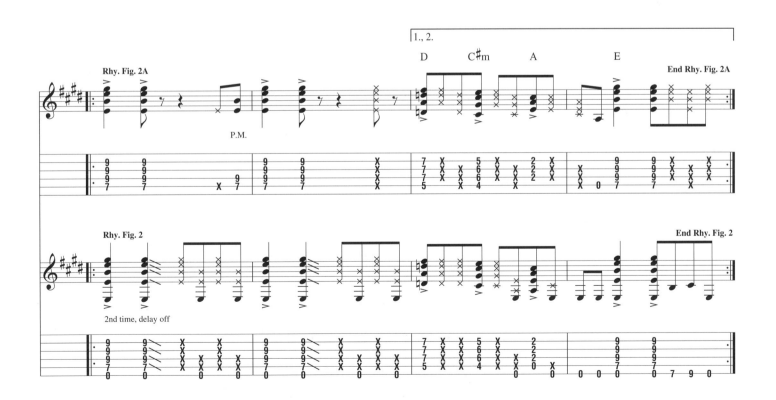

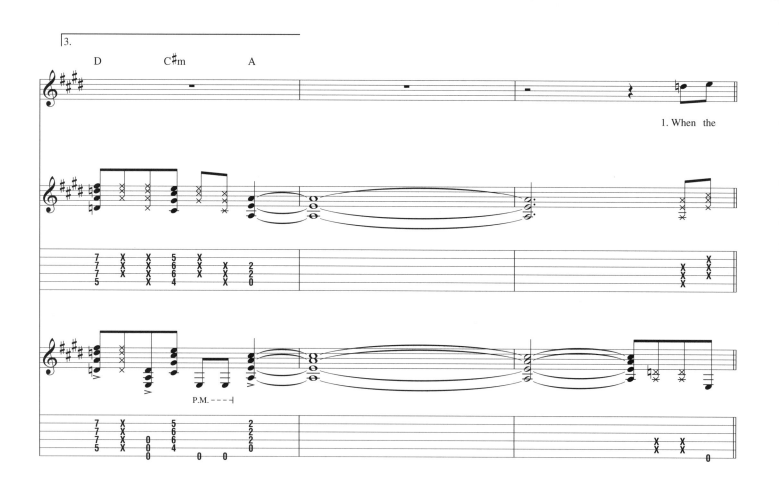

**Verse**

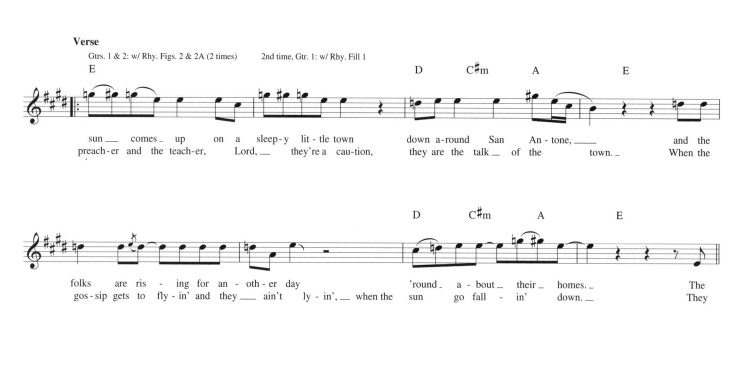

Rhy. Fill 1

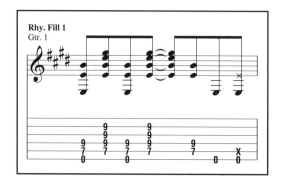

*Bkgd. gang vocs., next 5 meas.

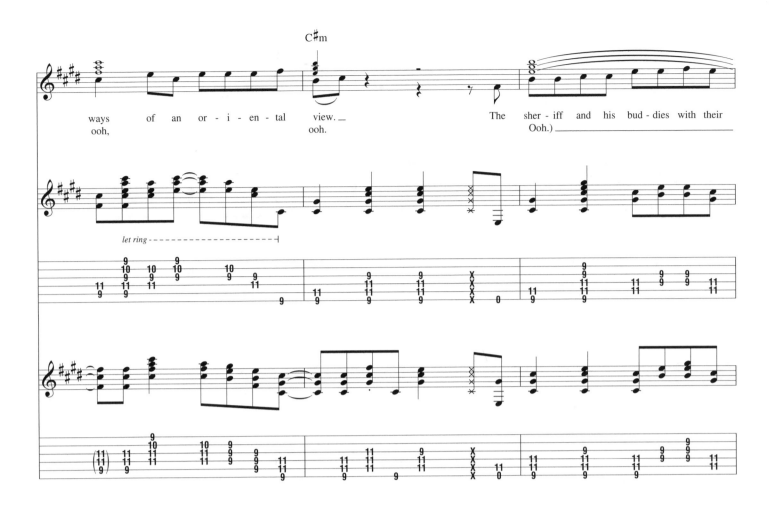

ways of an or - i - en - tal view. ___ The sher - iff and his bud - dies with their
ooh, ooh. Ooh.) _____

sam - ur - ai swords, ___ you can e - ven hear the mu - sic at ___ night. ___

And though it's a part of the Lone Star State,
(Ooh, _____

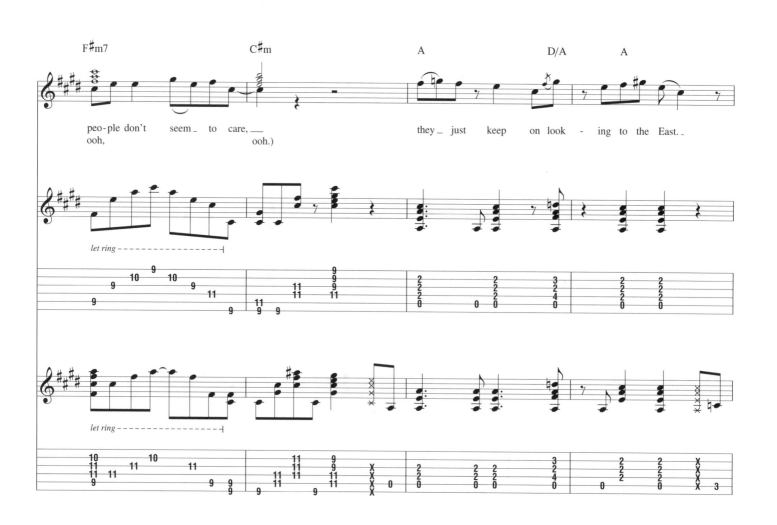

peo-ple don't seem to care, _____ they _ just keep on look - ing to the East. _
ooh, _____ ooh.)

Interlude

*Gtr. 1: w/ Rhy. Fig. 1
Gtr. 2 tacet

*w/ delay

**Gtrs. 1 & 2: w/ Rhy. Figs. 2 & 2A

**Gtr. 2: w/ dist.

Guitar Solo

***Gtrs. 1 & 2

Gtr. 1, delay off

***Composite arrangement

from Van Morrison - *His Band and the Street Choir*

# Domino

**Words and Music by Van Morrison**

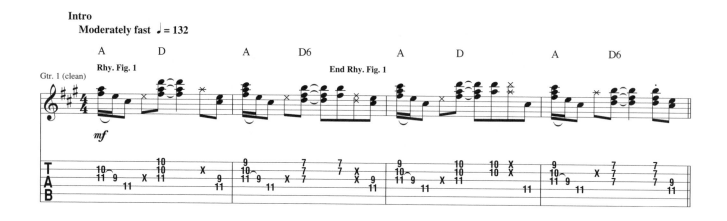

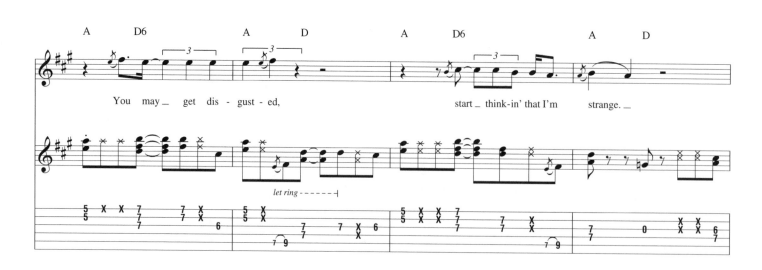

That __ case, I'll go un-der-ground, __ get __ some heav-y rest.

Nev-er __ have to wor-ry a-bout what is worst __ and what is best. __ Jih!

**Chorus**

Oh, oh, dom-i-no. All right. Roll me o-ver, Ro-me-o. There __ you go. __

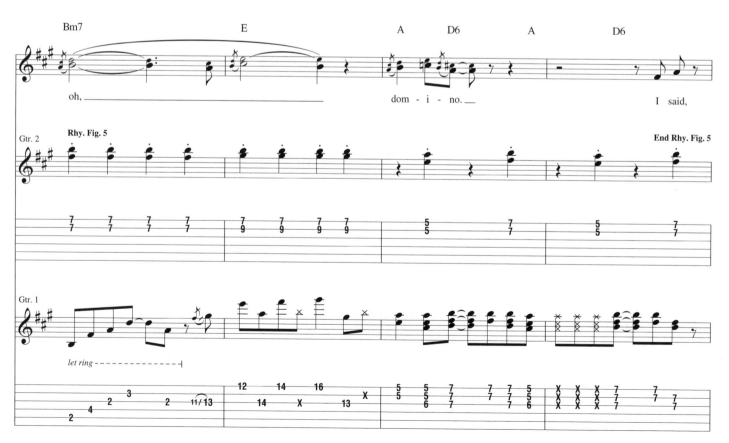

Gtr. 2: w/ Rhy. Fig. 8 (4 times)

Lord, have mer-cy.    I said    oh,    oh,    dom-i-no.

Roll me o-ver, Ro-me-o.    There_ you go. _    Yeah,    all right,    say it a-gain.

Oh, _____    dom-i-no. _    Hey!  Hey!  I said

oh, _____    dom-i-no. _

# Dream On

### Words and Music by Steven Tyler

**Intro**

Moderately slow ♩ = 78

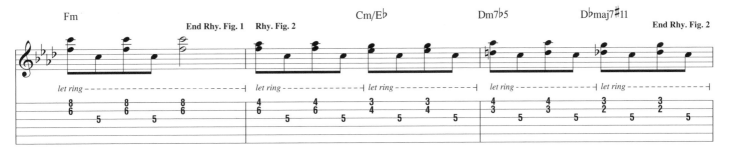

*Chord symbols reflect implied harmony.

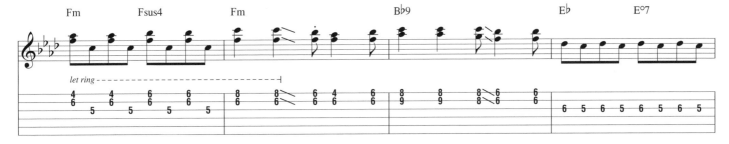

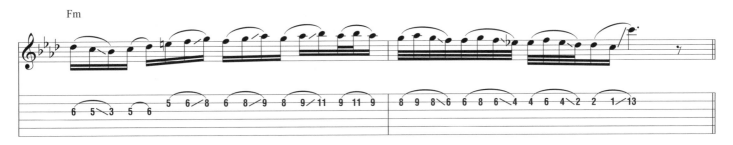

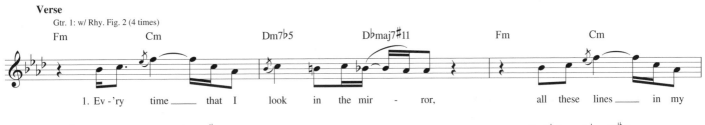

**Verse**

Gtr. 1: w/ Rhy. Fig. 2 (4 times)

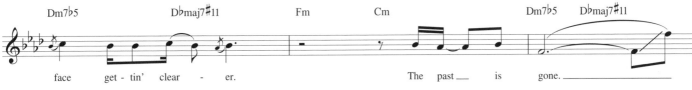

1. Ev-'ry time ____ that I look in the mir - ror, all these lines ____ in my face get-tin' clear - er. The past ____ is gone. ____

It went by like ___ dusk to dawn. ___

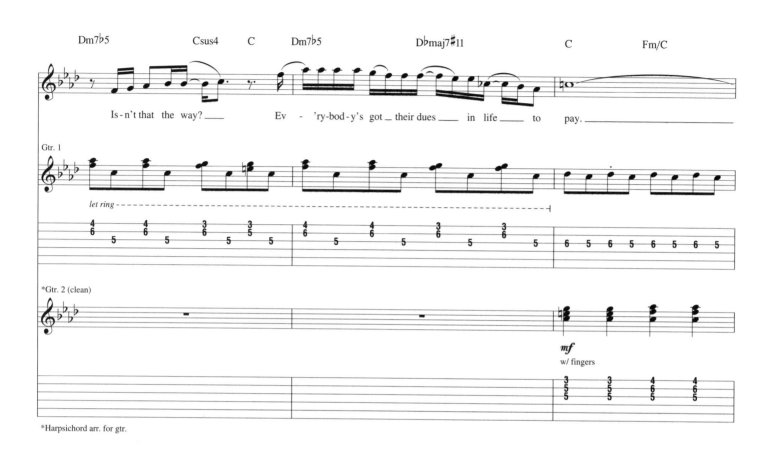

Is-n't that the way? ___ Ev - 'ry-bod-y's got ___ their dues ___ in life ___ to pay. ___

*Harpsichord arr. for gtr.

**Pre-Chorus**

___ Well, ___ I know no-bod-y knows where it comes ___ and where ___ it goes. ___

**Pre-Chorus**

Hey, _____ oh. _____ Mm. _

**Chorus**

Gtr. 4 tacet

Dream on, __ 'n' dream on, __ 'n' dream on, __ dream your-self a dream come

*See top of first page of song for chord diagrams pertaining to rhythm slashes.

true. _____

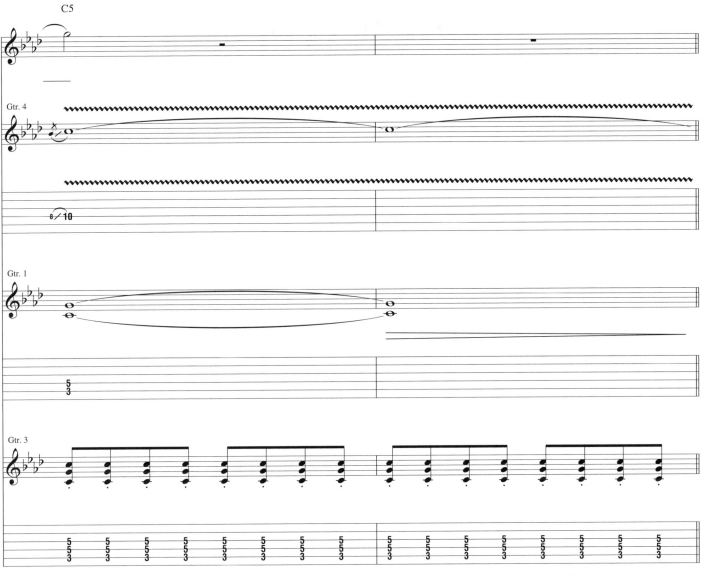

*Microphonic fdbk., not caused by string vibration.*

*Begin fade*

*Fade out*

**Outro**

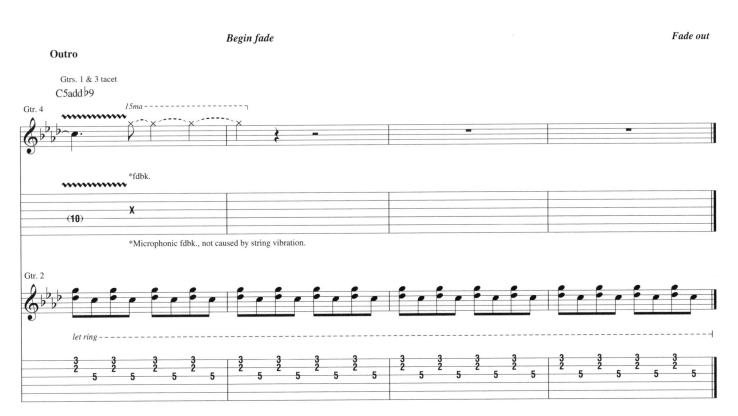

from Buffalo Springfield - *Buffalo Springfield*

# For What It's Worth

### Words and Music by Stephen Stills

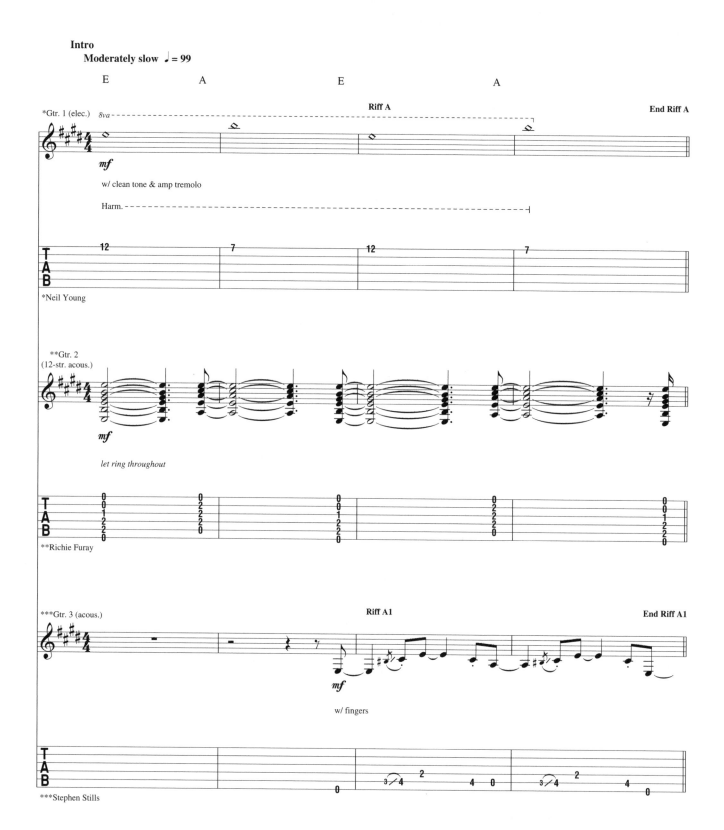

**Chorus**

stop.  Chil - dren, what's that sound? __ Ev - 'ry - bod - y look  what's  go - in'  down. _____

**Interlude**

**Verse**

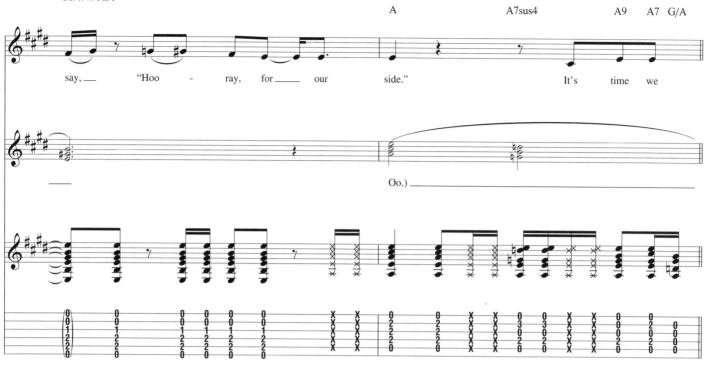

**Chorus**

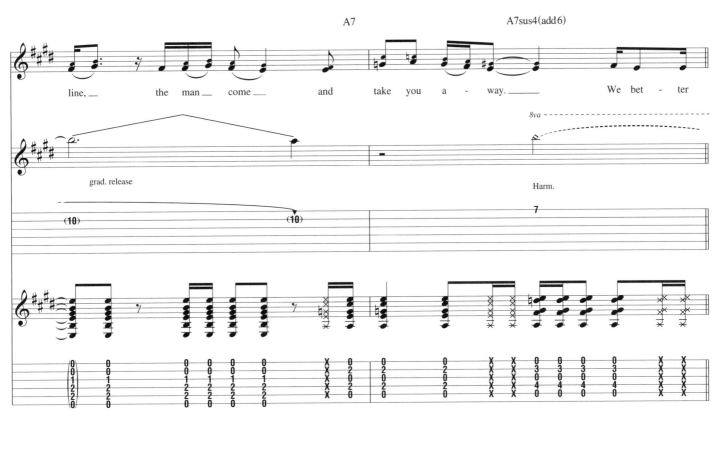

line,_____ the man___ come___ and take you a - way._____ We bet - ter

**Chorus**

stop.
(Stop,

Hey, ___ what's that sound? __
What's that sound? _

Ev - 'ry - bod - y look what's go - in'. We bet - ter
Ev - 'ry - bod - y look what's go - in' down.)

# Fortunate Son

**Words and Music by John Fogerty**

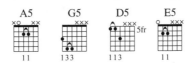

Tune down 1 step:
(low to high) D-G-C-F-A-D

*Chord symbols reflect overall harmony.

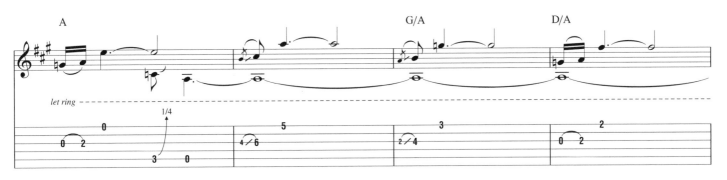

ooh, their red, white and blue. _____

And when the band _ plays "Hail _____ to the _ Chief," _ ooh, _ they point the can - non at

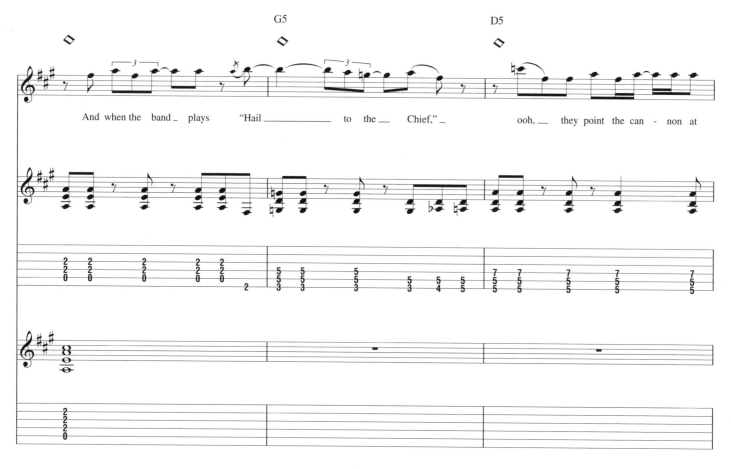

you,       Lord. ___               But it ain't   me, ___              it ain't me; _____

I   ain't  no  sen - a - tor's     son, ___            son. ___

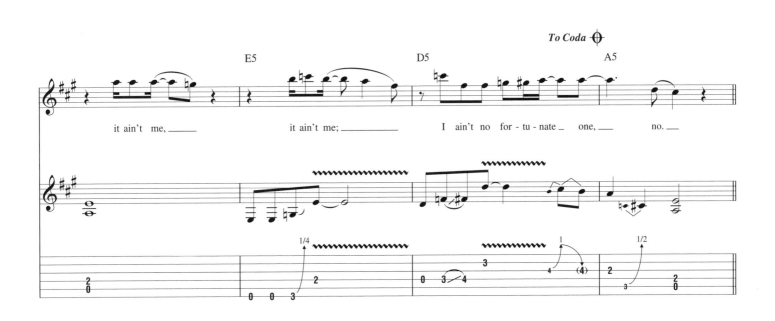

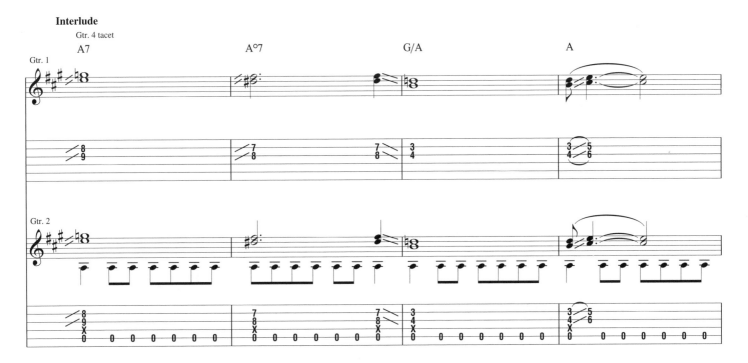

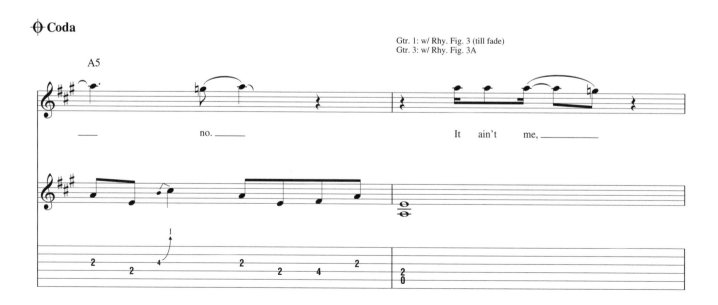

# Go Your Own Way

## Words and Music by Lindsey Buckingham

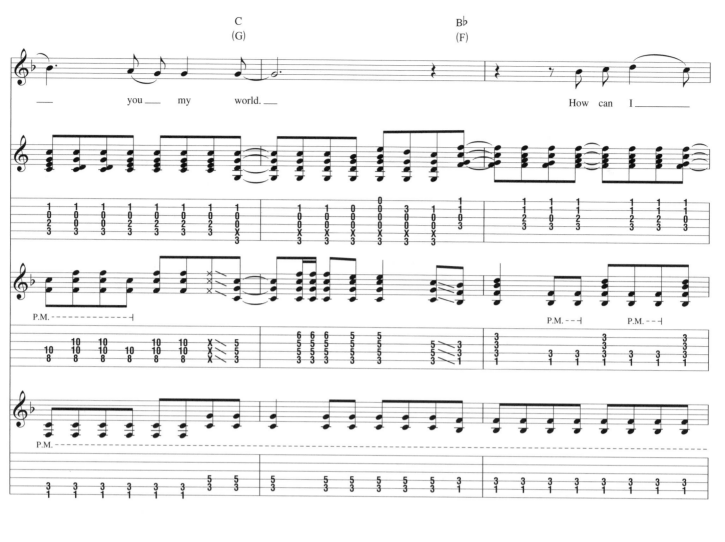

you ___ my world. ___                                    How can I ___

when you won't    take ___    it    from ___   me? ___

End Rhy. Fig. 1B

(cont. in slashes)

End Rhy. Fig. 1

End Rhy. Fig. 1A

**Verse**

Gtrs. 1, 2 & 3: / Rhy. Figs. 1, 1A & 1B

F
(C)

C
(G)

Bb
(F)

2. Tell me why ____ ev - 'ry - thing turned ____ a - round. ____

Gtr. 4 (elec.)

*p _____ mf

w/ slight dist.

13        (13)

*Vol. swell

Pack - ing up, ____ shack - ing up's all ____ you wan - na do. ____

10

If I could, ____ ba - by, I'd give ____ you ____ my world. ____

F
(C)

C
(G)

Bb
(F)

mf

fdbk.

10        (10)        (10)

***D.S. al Coda***

Gtr. 4 tacet

F
(C)

O - pen up, ____ ev - 'ry - thing's wait - ing for ____ you. ____

**

10        (10)

**Vol. swell

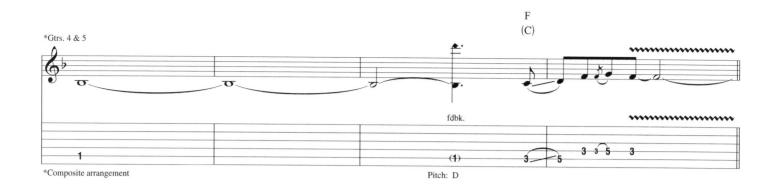

*Gtrs. 4 & 5

*Composite arrangement

F
(C)

fdbk.

Pitch: D

### Chorus

Gtrs. 1 & 2: w/ Rhy. Fig. 2 (4 times)
Gtr. 3: w/ Rhy. Fig. 2A (4 times)

Gtr. 5 tacet

Dm
(Am)

B♭
(F)

C
(G)

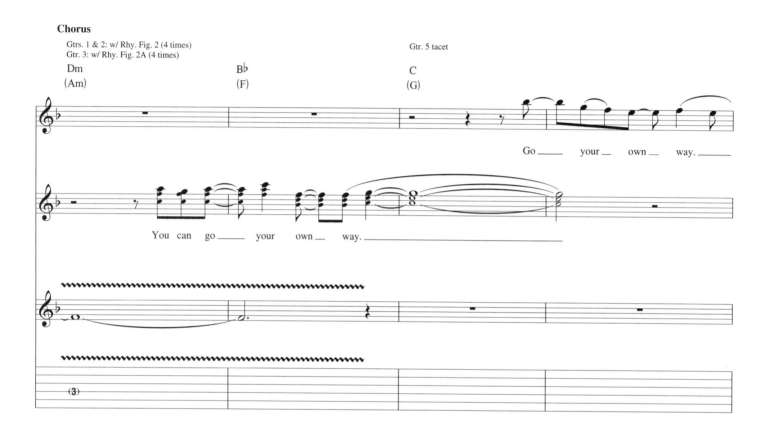

Go ___ your ___ own ___ way. ___

You can go ___ your own ___ way. ___

Dm
(Am)

B♭
(F)

C
(G)

An - oth - er lone - ly ___

You can call ___ it an - oth - er lone - ly day. ___

Gtr. 4

8va

mf

Outro-Guitar Solo

Gtrs. 1 & 2: w/ Rhy. Fig. 2 (till fade)
Gtr. 3: / Rhy. Fig. 2A (till fade)

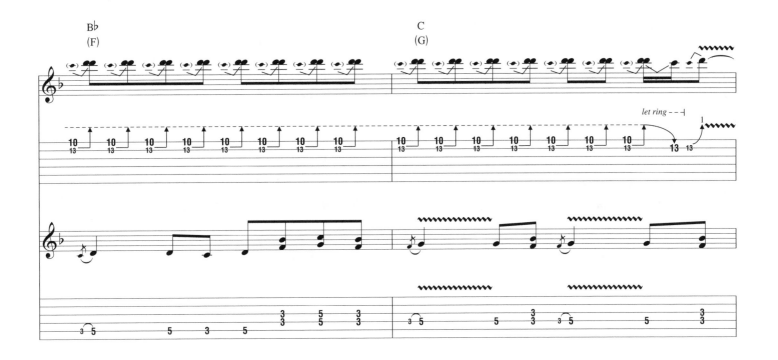

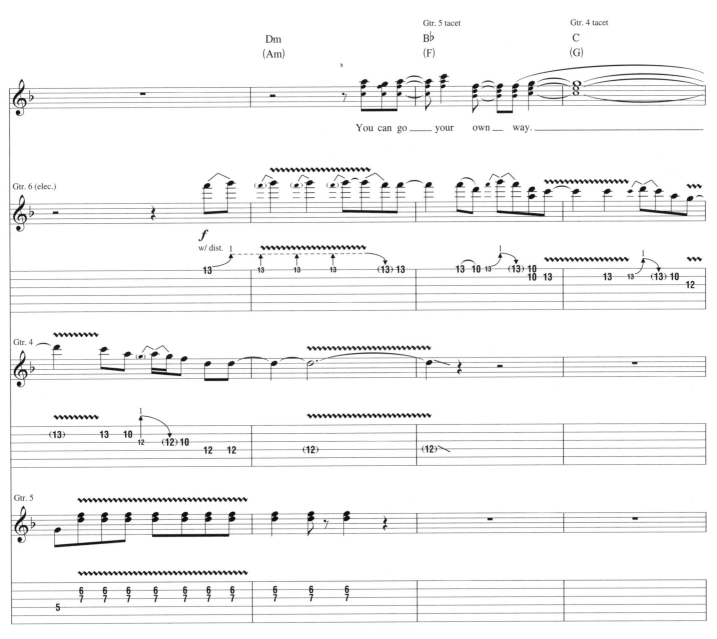

You can go ___ your ___ own ___ way. ___

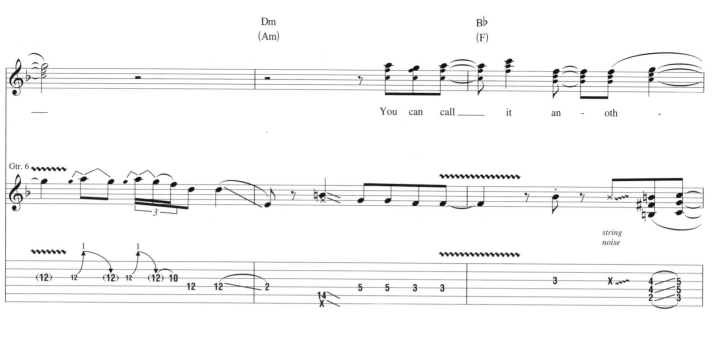

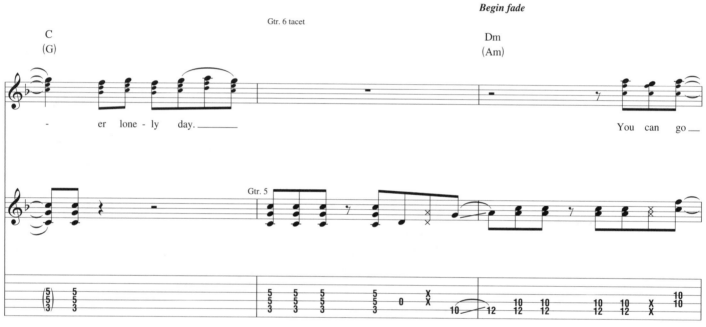

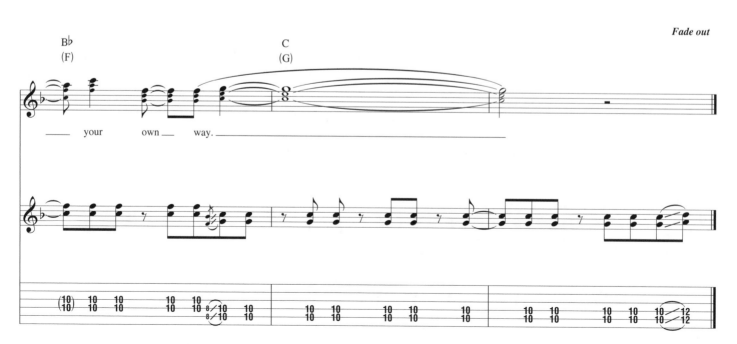

from BLIND FAITH - *Blind Faith*

# Had to Cry Today

## Words and Music by Steve Winwood

*Chord symbols reflect implied harmony.

**Verse**

al - read - y writ - ten that to - day will be one _____ to re - mem-

*let ring* - - - - - - - - - - - - -        w/ pick & finger
*let ring* - - - - - - - - - - - - -

**Riff B**

*let ring* - - - - - - - - - - - - -        *let ring* - - - - - - - - - - - - -

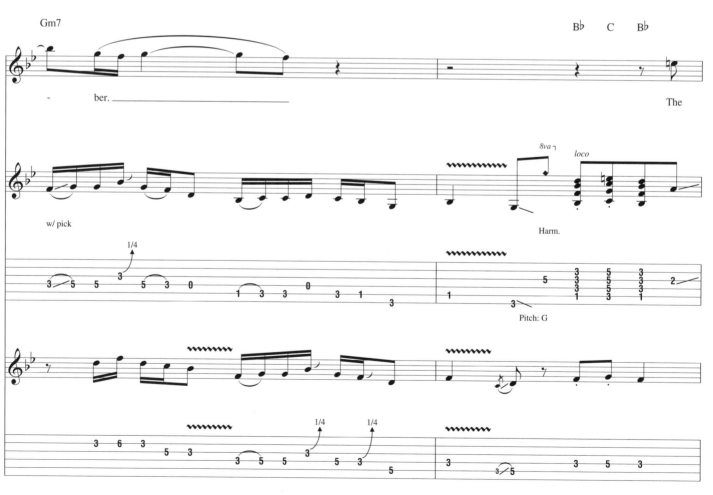

- ber. _____                                                The

w/ pick                                        Harm.

Pitch: G

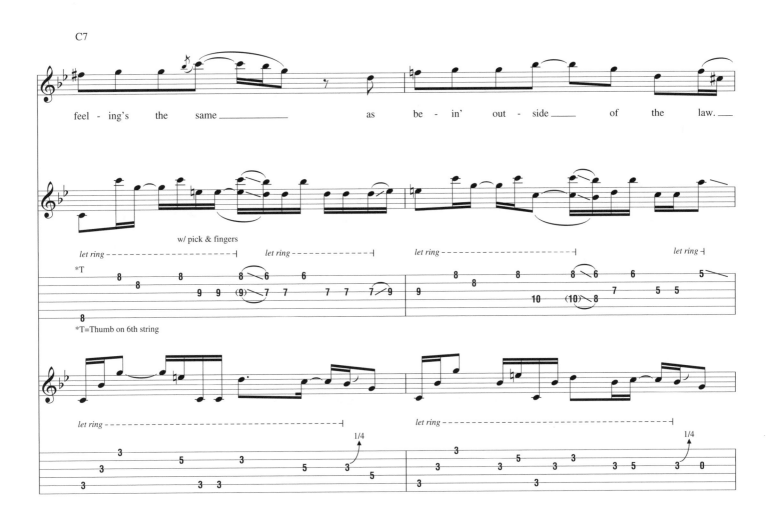

feel - ing's the same _____ as be - in' out - side _____ of the law. _____

w/ pick & fingers

*T

*T=Thumb on 6th string

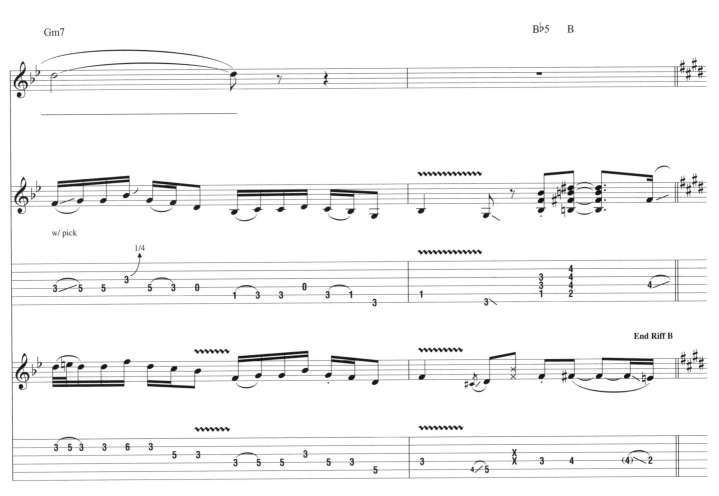

w/ pick

End Riff B

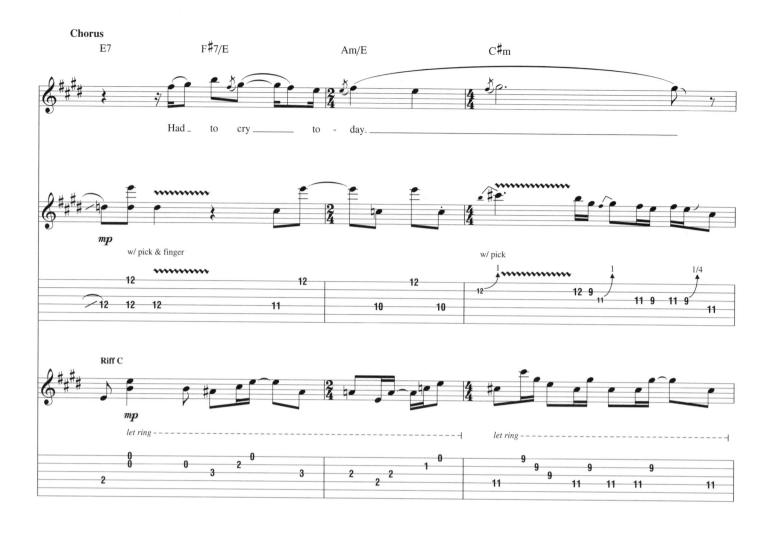

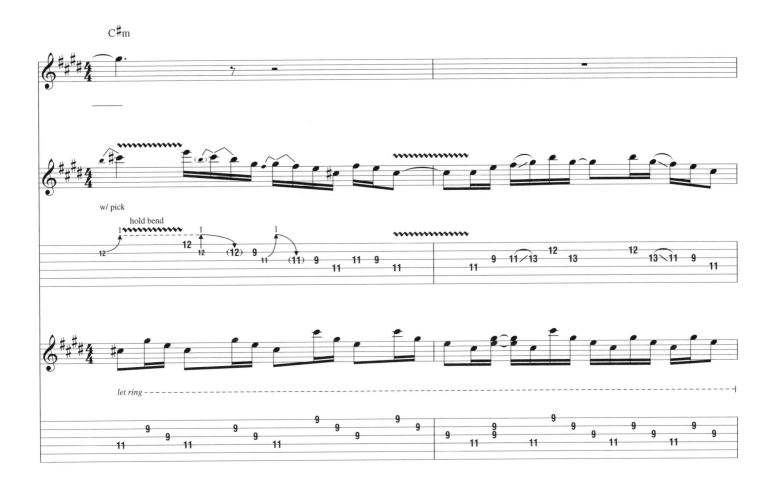

**Interlude**

Gtrs. 1 & 2: w/ Riffs A & A1 (2 times)

2. I'm

**Chorus**

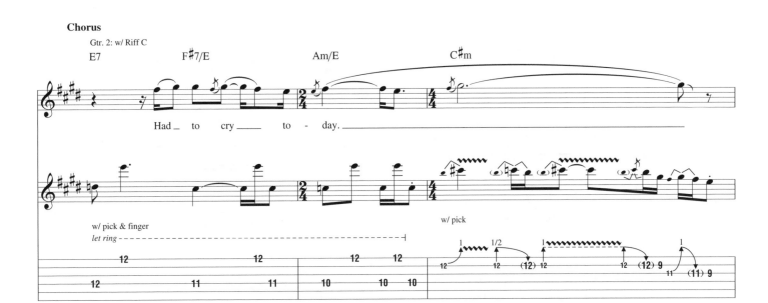

Had _ to cry _ to - day. _

Well, I _____ saw _ your sign _____ and I missed _____ you there. _

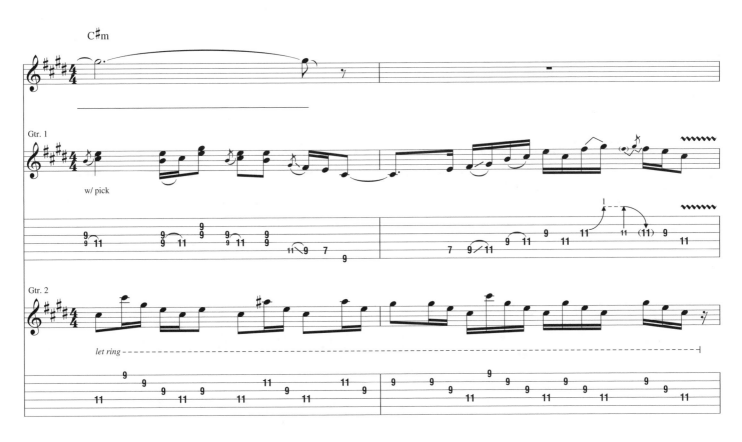

And I missed you ___ there. ___

**Interlude**

Gtr. 1: w/ Riff A
Gtr. 2: w/ Riff A1 (2 times)

**Guitar Solo**

Gtr. 2: w/ Riff A1 (14 times)

## Interlude

Gtr. 1: w/ Riff A (2 times)
Gtr. 2: w/ Riff A1

Riff D

3. It's

End Riff D

## Verse

Gtr. 2: w/ Riff B

al - read - y writ - ten that to - day will be one ___ to re - mem -

Gtr. 1

let ring

ber. ___

The

feel - ing's the same _____ as be - ing out - side _____ of the law. _____

**Chorus**

Gtr. 2: w/ Riff C (1st 3 meas.)

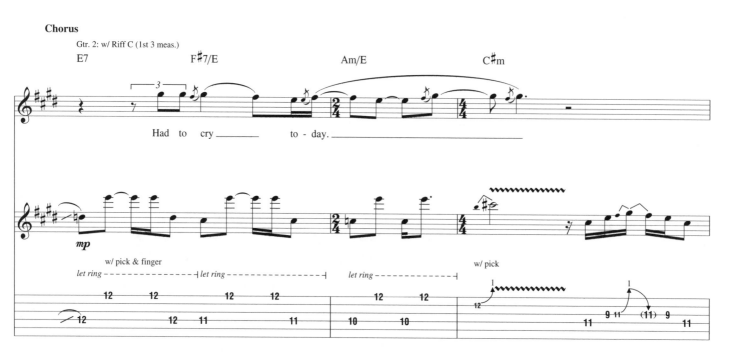

Had to cry _____ to - day.

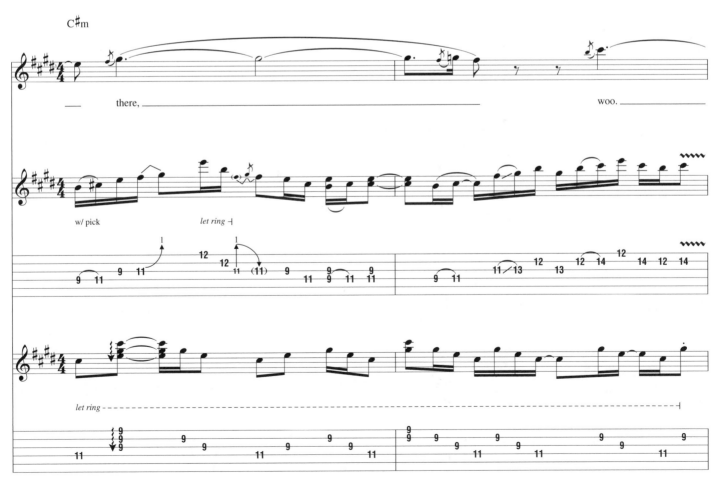

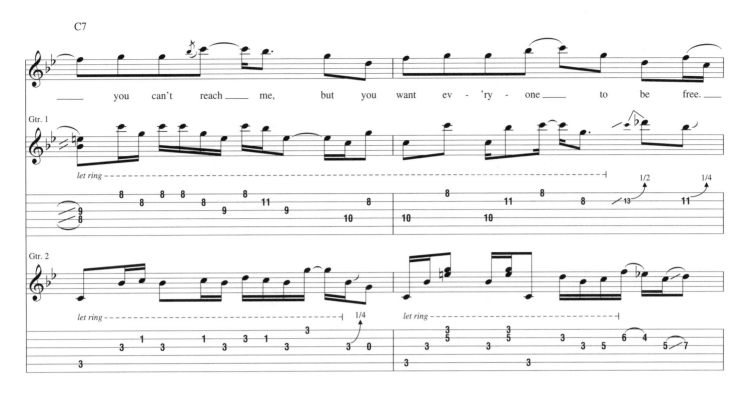

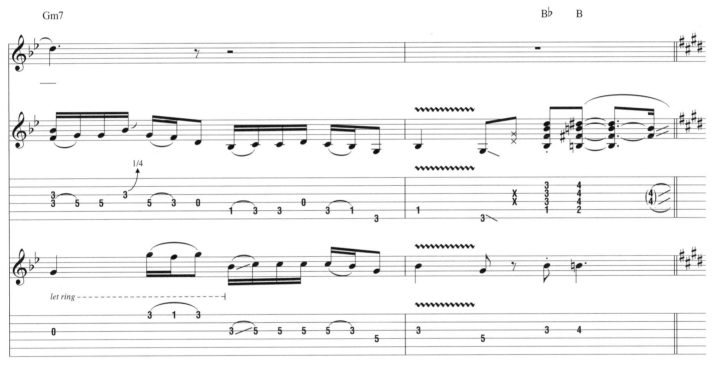

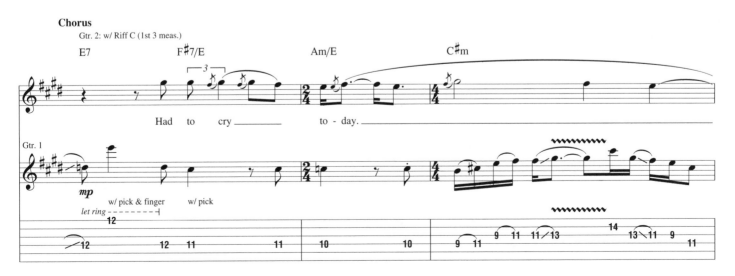

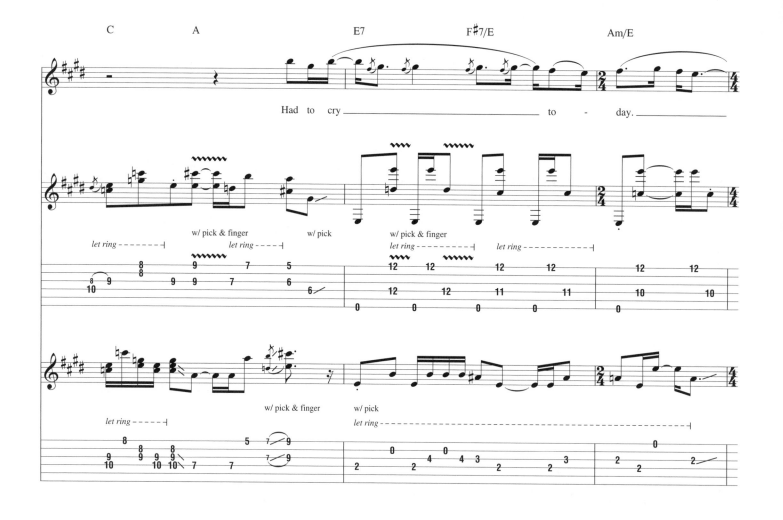

Had to cry _____ to - day. _____

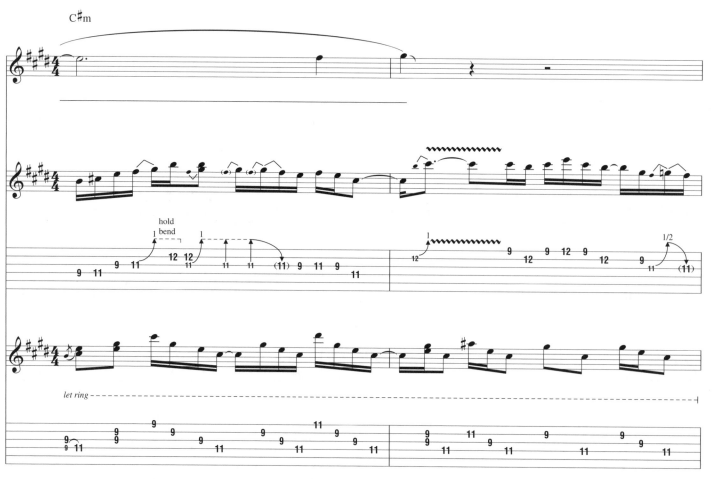

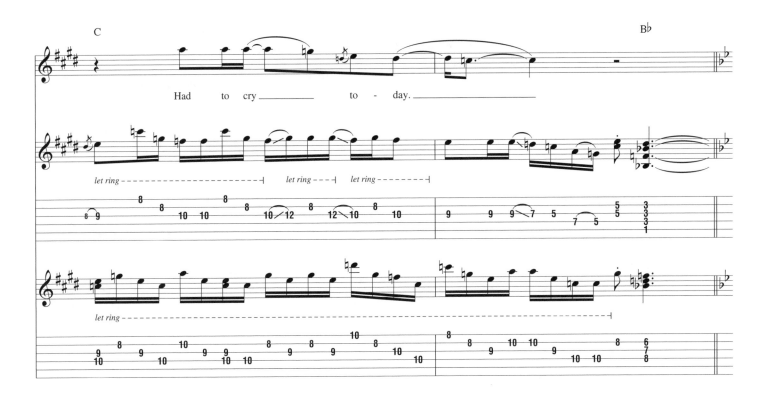

Had to cry ____ to - day. ____

**Guitar Solo**

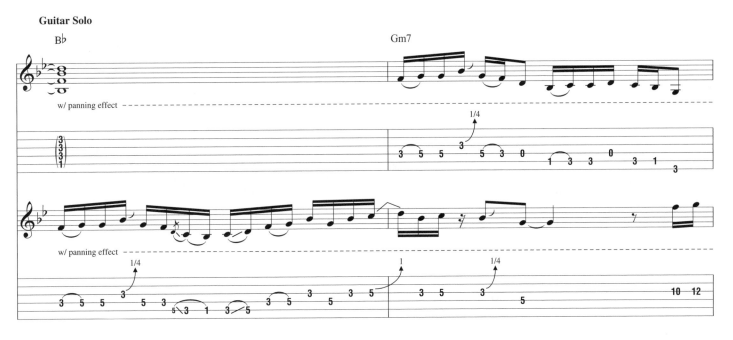

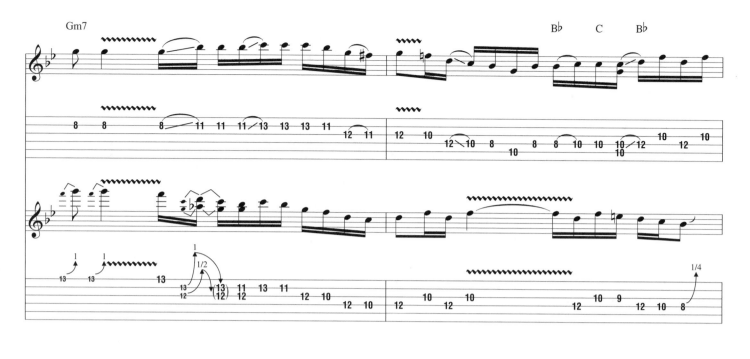

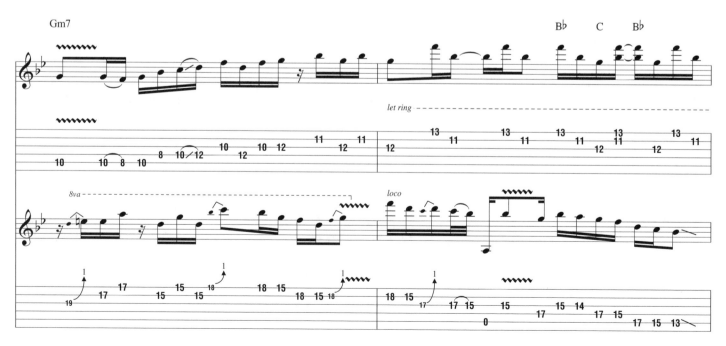

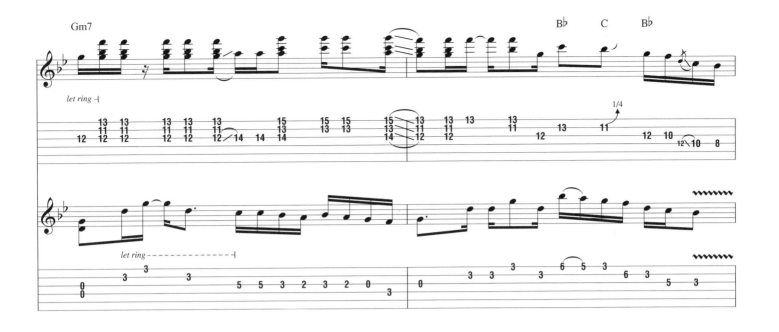

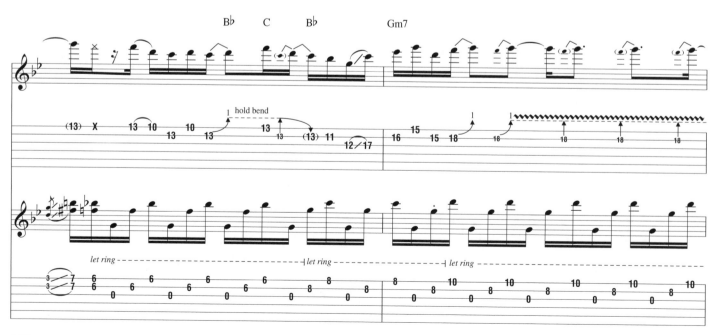

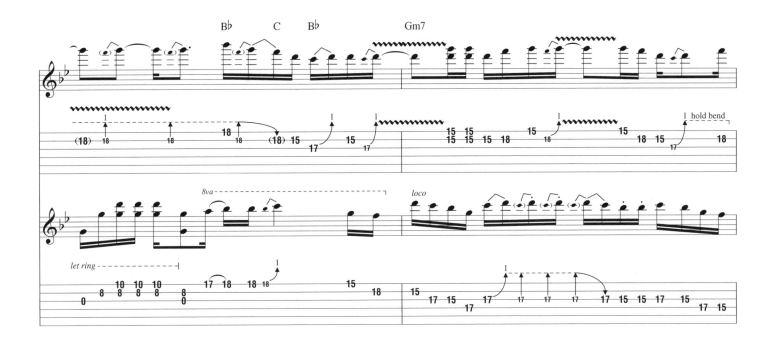

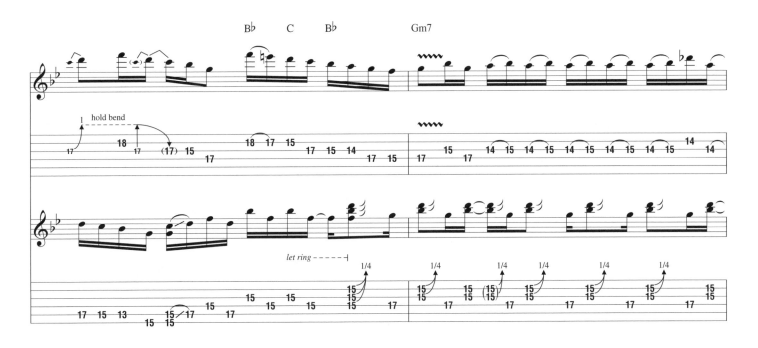

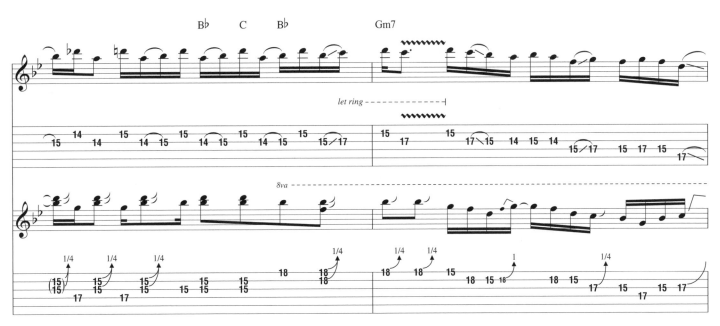

**Outro**
Gtr. 1: w/ Riff A (2 times)
Gtr. 2: w/ Riff D (2 times)

from The Georgia Satellites - *Georgia Satellites*

# Keep Your Hands to Yourself

**Words and Music by Daniel Baird**

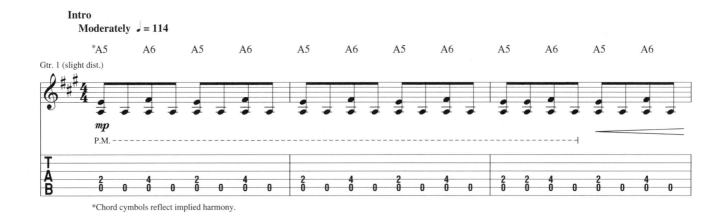

*Chord cymbols reflect implied harmony.

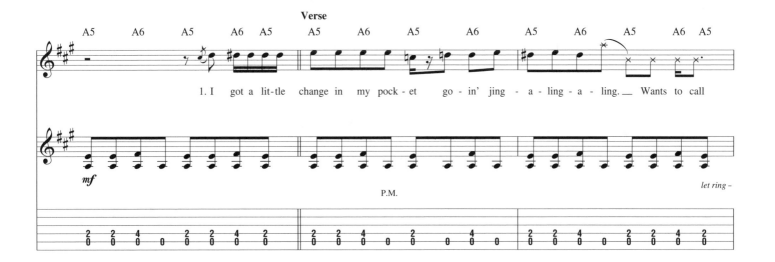

1. I got a lit-tle change in my pock-et go-in' jing - a - ling - a - ling.___ Wants to call

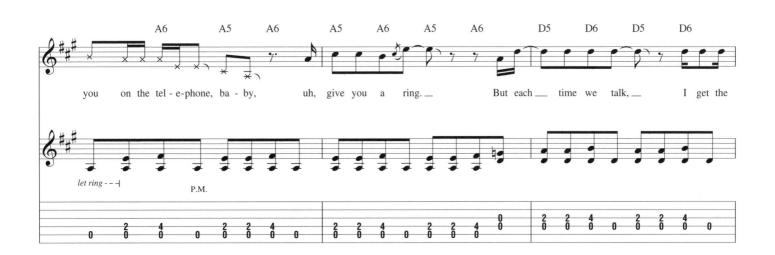

you on the tel-e-phone, ba - by, uh, give you a ring.___ But each___ time we talk,___ I get the

same old thing. Al - ways, "No hug - gie, no kiss - ie un - til I get a _____ wed - din' ring." ___ My

hon - ey, my ba - by, don't put my love up - on no shelf. She said, "Don't

hand me no lines _____ and keep your hands to your - self." _____

Gtr. 3 (dist.)

Gtr. 1

Gtr. 2 (slight dist.)

hand me no lines _____ and keep your hands to your - self." _____

*Chord symbols reflect basic harmony.

Oh, go, man, _____ go!

End Rhy. Fig. 2

Gtr. 2: w/ Rhy. Fig. 2

Gtr. 3

Gtr. 1

**Outro-Guitar Solo**

Gtr. 2: w/ Rhy. Fig. 2 (till fade)

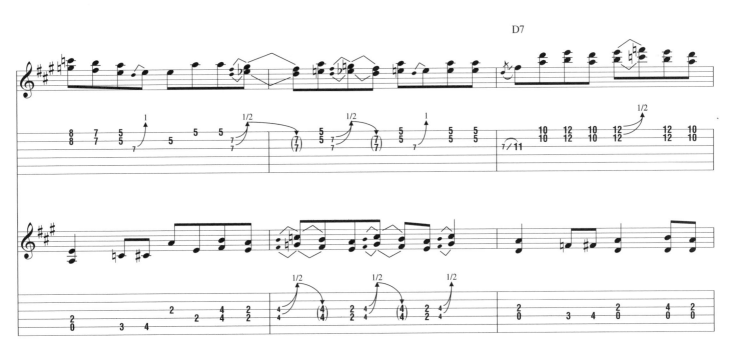

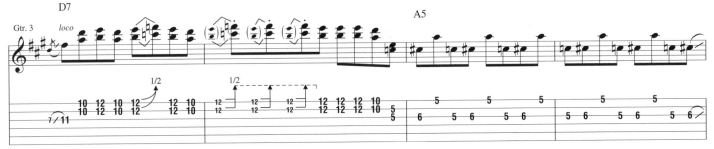

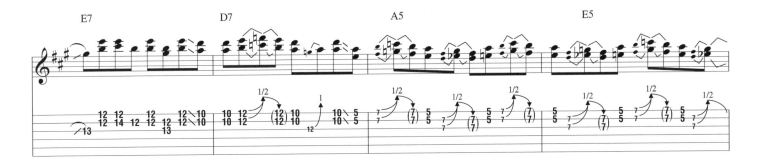

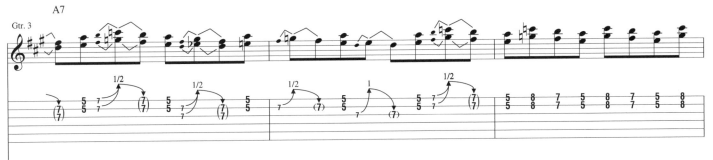

# Life in the Fast Lane

### Words and Music by Don Henley, Glenn Frey and Joe Walsh

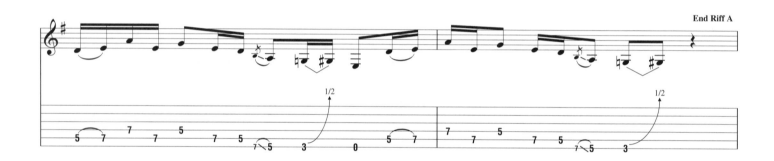

Gtr. 1 tacet

*Em7

Riff C

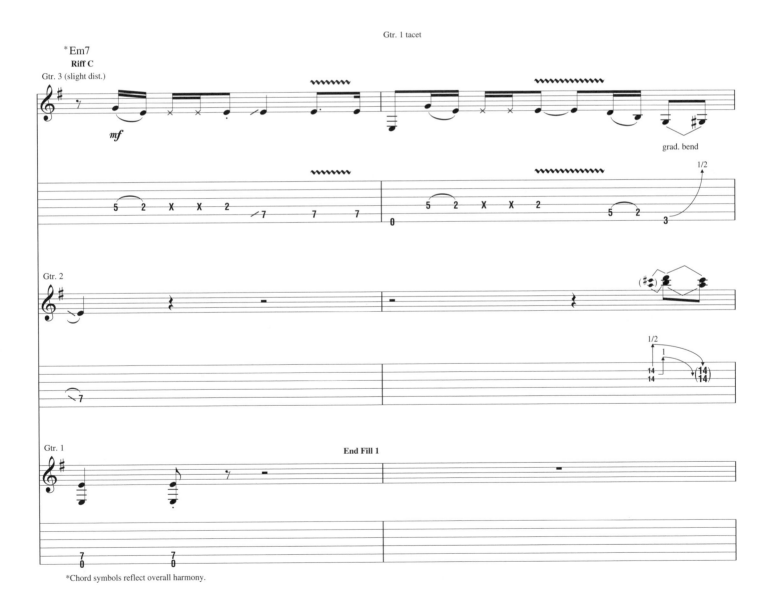

*Chord symbols reflect overall harmony.

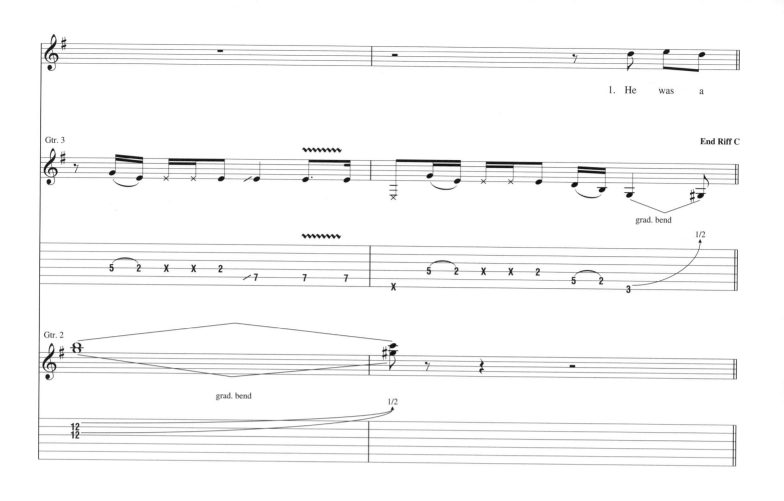

1. He was a

Gtr. 3

End Riff C

grad. bend

Gtr. 2

grad. bend

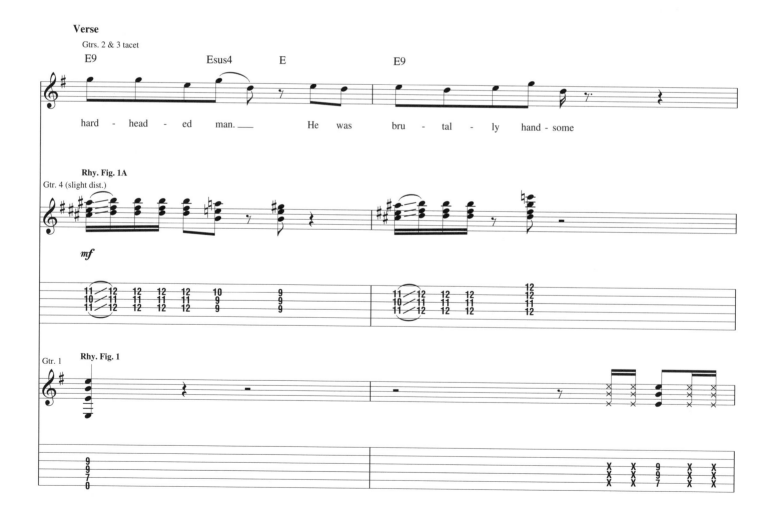

**Verse**

Gtrs. 2 & 3 tacet

E9          Esus4    E          E9

hard - head - ed man. ___    He was   bru - tal - ly   hand - some

**Rhy. Fig. 1A**

Gtr. 4 (slight dist.)

*mf*

Gtr. 1     **Rhy. Fig. 1**

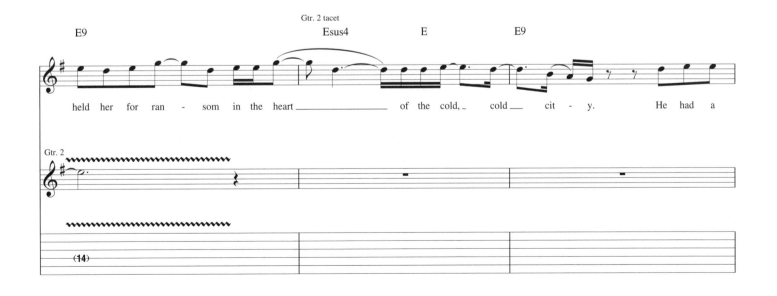

nas - ty rep - u - ta - tion as a cru - el dude. ___ They said he was ruth - less. They

said he was crude. ___ They had one thing in com - mon, they were good in bed. ___ She'd say, ___

**Chorus**

Gtr. 1: w/ Riff A (1st 3 meas.)
Gtr. 4 tacet

Gtr. 1: w/ Fill 1

N.C.

(Life in the fast __ lane. Sure-ly make __ you lose your mind. __ Life in the fast __ lane.) Yeah. __

**Interlude**

Gtr. 3: w/ Riff C

Em7

*Spoken:* Are you with me so far?

Gtr. 2

**Verse**

Gtrs. 1 & 4: w/ Rhy. Figs. 1 & 1A (2 times)

E9      Esus4   E      E9                          Esus4   E

2. Ea - ger for ac - tion and hot for the game. __ The com - ing at - trac - tion, the

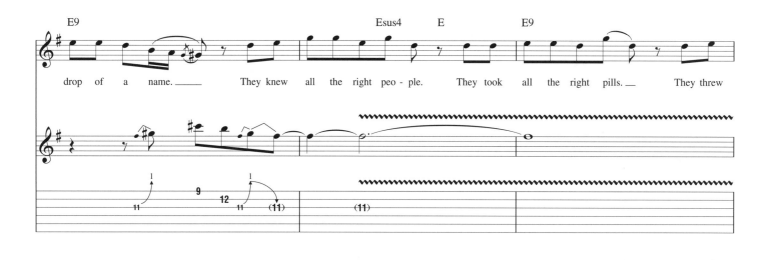

drop of a name. _____ They knew all the right peo - ple. They took all the right pills. _____ They threw

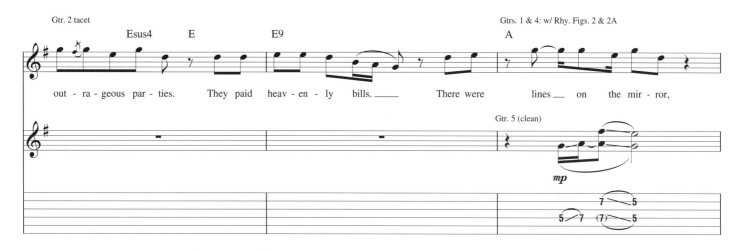

out - ra - geous par - ties. They paid heav - en - ly bills. _____ There were lines _____ on the mir - ror,

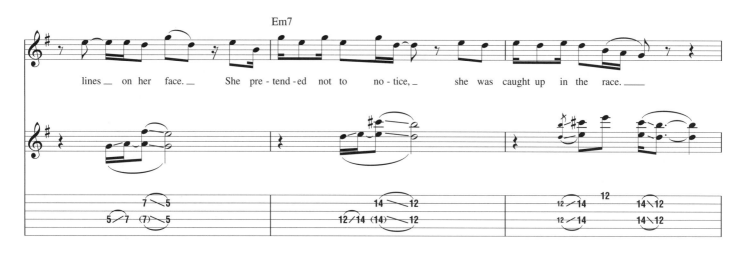

lines _____ on her face. _____ She pre - tend - ed not to no - tice, _____ she was caught up in the race. _____

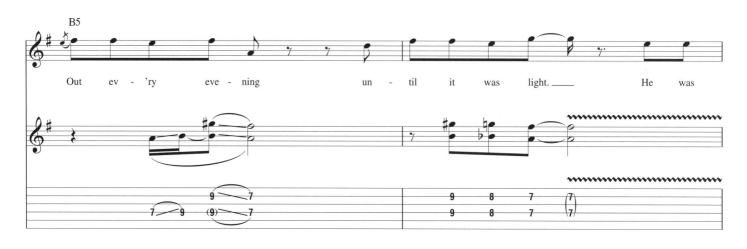

Out ev - 'ry eve - ning un - til it was light. _____ He was

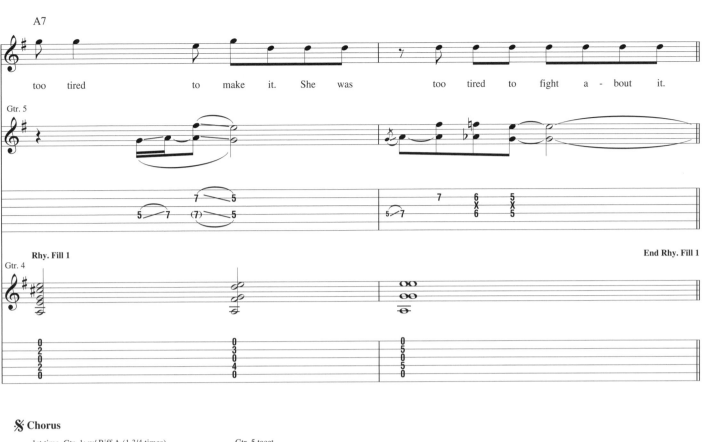

too tired to make it. She was too tired to fight a-bout it.

*Gtr. 5*

**Rhy. Fill 1** **End Rhy. Fill 1**

*Gtr. 4*

*𝄋* **Chorus**

1st time, Gtr. 1: w/ Riff A (1 3/4 times)
1st time, Gtr. 4 tacet
2nd time, Gtr. 1: w/ Riff A (2 times)
2nd time, Gtr. 2: w/ Riff B
2nd time, Gtr. 8 tacet

Gtr. 5 tacet

N.C.

(Life in the fast _ lane.   Sure - ly make _ you lose _ your mind. _   Life in the fast _ lane.

*Gtr. 5*

*To Coda* ⊕

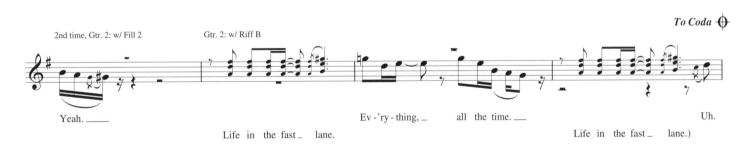

2nd time, Gtr. 2: w/ Fill 2     Gtr. 2: w/ Riff B

Yeah. _     Ev -'ry-thing, _   all the time. _   Uh.
Life in the fast _ lane.                         Life in the fast _ lane.)

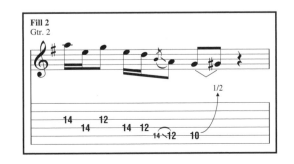

**Fill 2**
*Gtr. 2*

**Guitar Solo**

Gtr. 2 tacet

B

*Doubled throughout

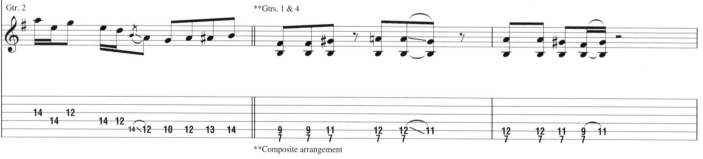

**Composite arrangement

162

**Outro-Guitar Solo**

Gtr. 3: w/ Riff C (till fade)   Gtr. 1 tacet

Gtr. 4 tacet

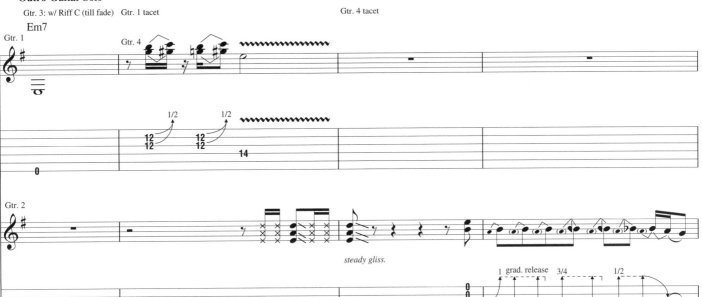

Gtr. 1: w/ Rhy. Fig. 4 (till fade)

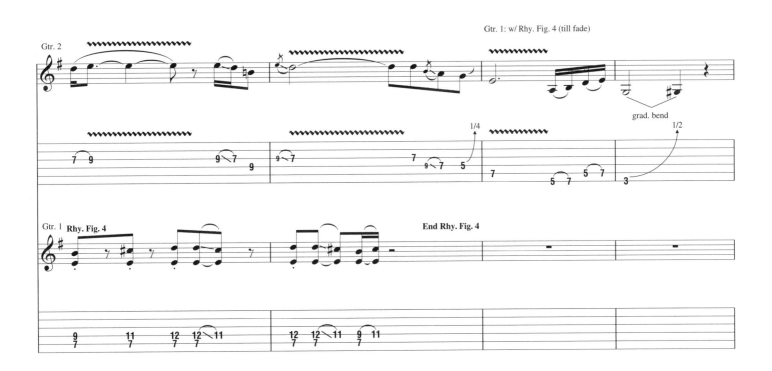

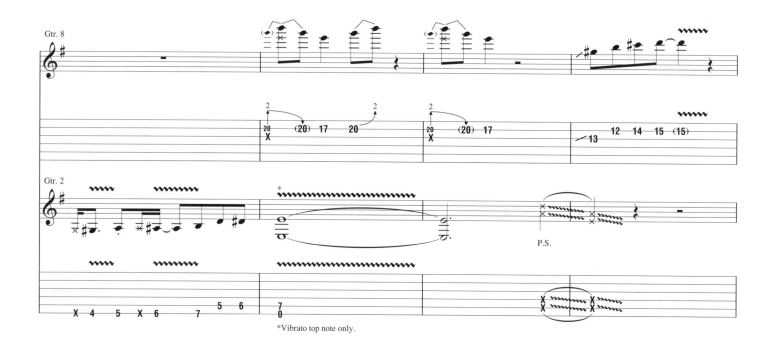

*Vibrato top note only.

**Begin fade**

Gtr. 8 tacet

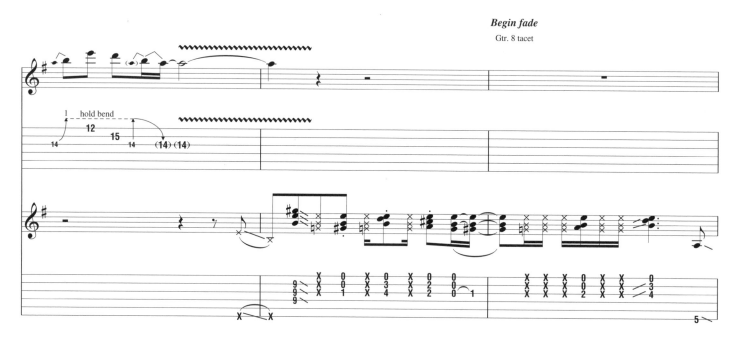

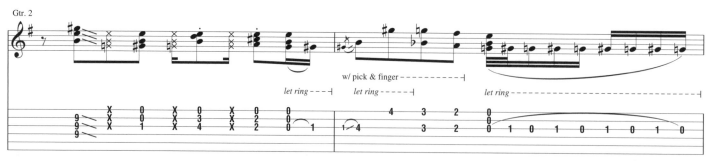

**Fade out**

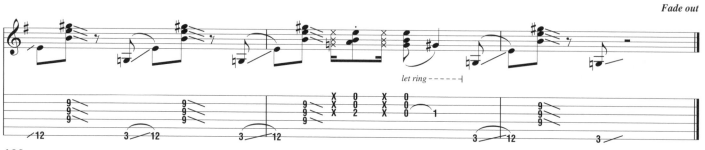

from Journey - *Infinity*

# Lights

### Words and Music by Neal Schon and Steve Perry

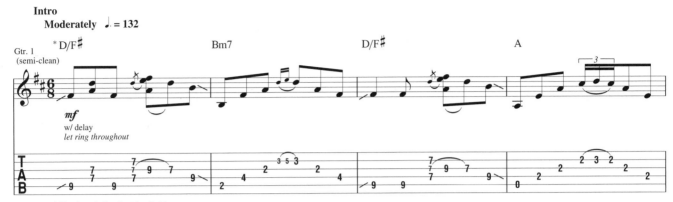

*Chord symbols reflect implied harmony.

sun    shines    on       the    bay, _____         ooh,  I

wan - na  be  there _____        in  my ___ cit - y, ___      oh. ___

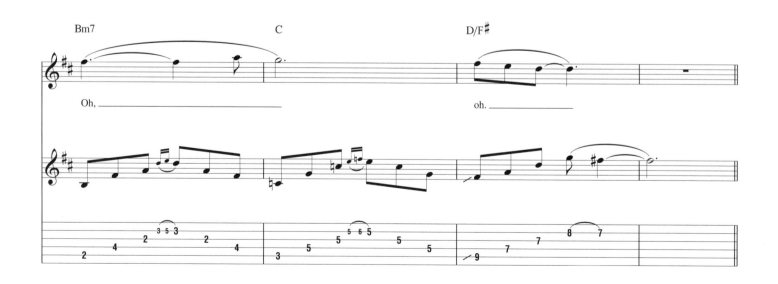

Oh, _____         oh. _____

Verse

D/F#   Bm   C

1. So you think you're ___ lone - ly, ___

Gtr. 2 (dist.)

*mf*

Gtr. 1

D/F#   Gtr. 2 tacet   Bm   C

well, my ___ friend, ___ I'm lone - ly too. ___

D/F#   Bm   C

I wan - na get back ___ to my cit - y ___ by the bay. ___

Gtr. 1  **Riff B**                                          **End Riff B**

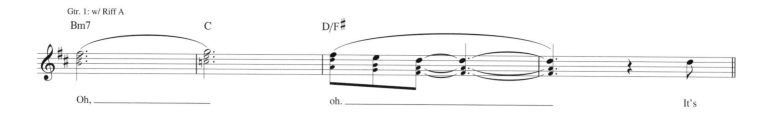

Bridge

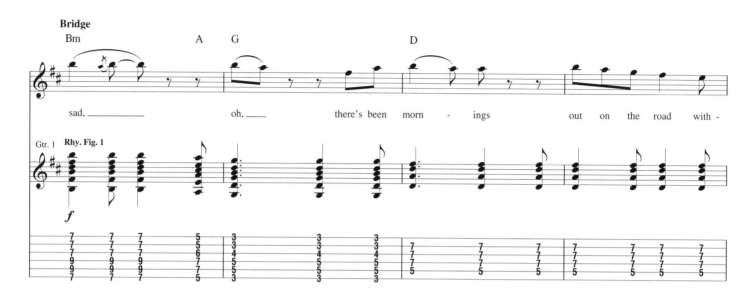

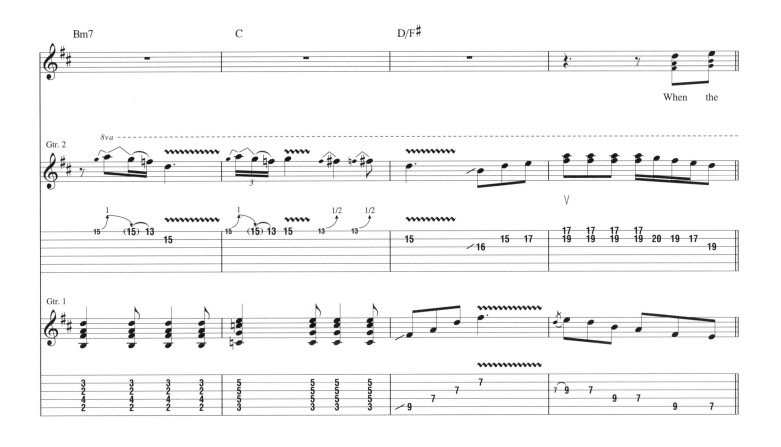

## Chorus

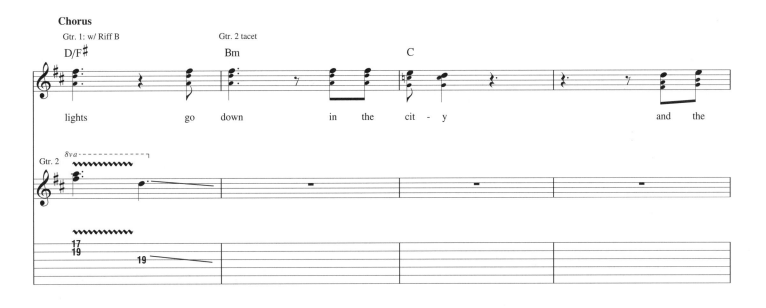

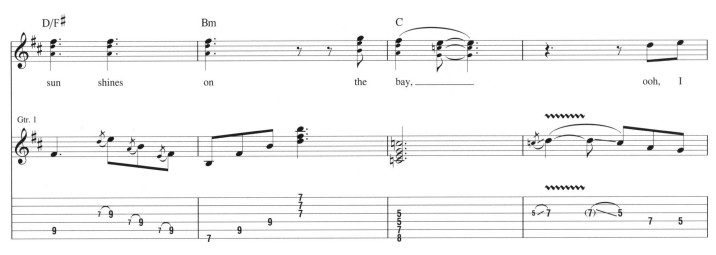

from The Police - *Reggatta De Blanc*

# Message in a Bottle

## Words and Music by Sting

**Intro**

**Fast** ♩ = 150

**Verse**

Gtrs. 1 & 2: w/ Riffs A & A1 (8 times)

1. Just a cast - a - way, __ an is - land lost __ at sea, __ oh. __

An - oth - er lone - ly day, __ no one here but me, __ oh. __

More lone - li - ness __ than an - y man __ could bear. __

Res - cue me __ be - fore __ I fall __ in - to des - pair, __ oh. __

**Pre-Chorus**

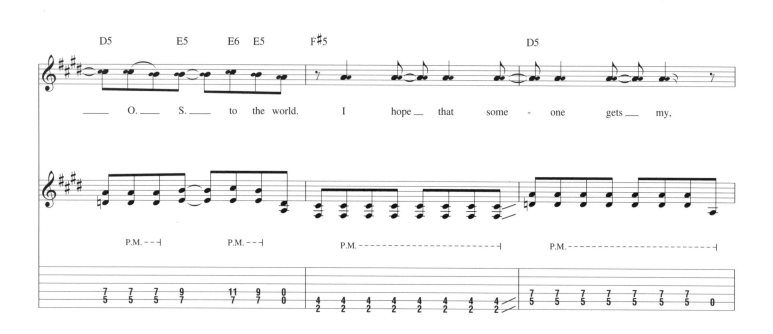

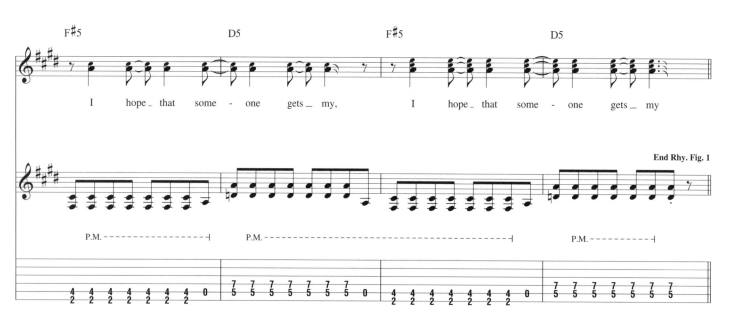

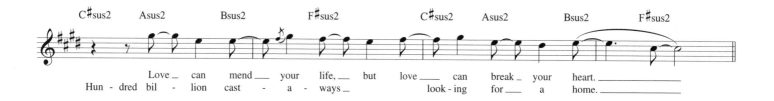

Love_ can mend_ your life, but love_ can break_ your heart._

Hun - dred bil - lion cast - a - ways_ look - ing for_ a home._

**Pre-Chorus**

Gtrs. 1 & 2: w/ Rhy. Fig. 1

2nd time, Gtr. 3: w/ Fill 1

I'll send_ an S._ O._ S._ to the world. I'll send_ an S._ O._ S._ to the world.

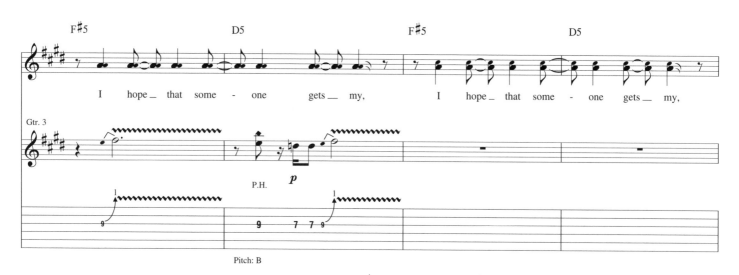

I hope_ that some - one gets_ my, I hope_ that some - one gets_ my,

Gtr. 3

P.H.

*p*

Pitch: B

*To Coda* ⊕

**Chorus**

Gtrs. 1 & 2: w/ Rhy. Fig. 2 (7 times)

I hope_ that some - one gets_ my mes - sage in_ a bot - tle,_ yeah.

*mp*

**Fill 1**

Gtr. 3

*p*

1/2              1/2              1/2              1/2

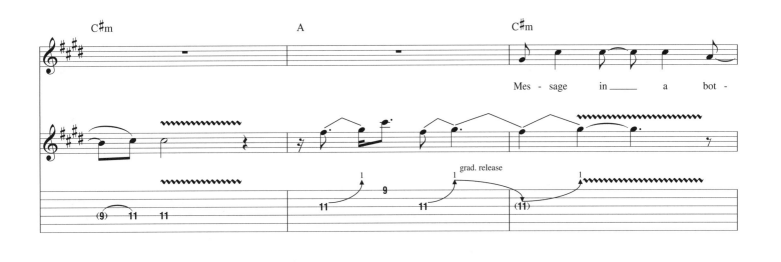

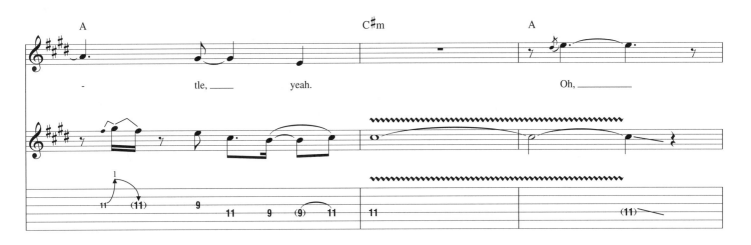

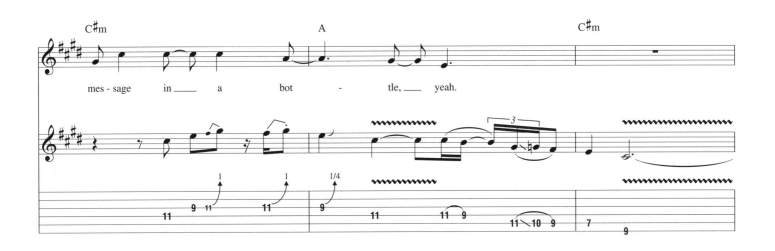

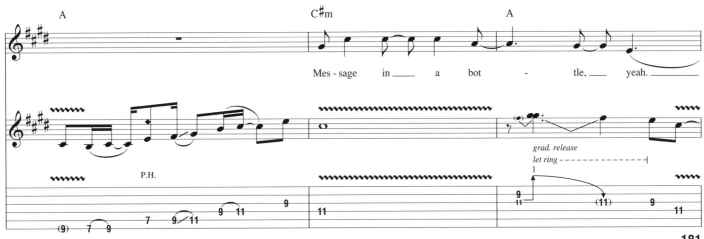

C#m A C#m A
Mes sage in a bot - tle, oh.
1/4 1/2
C#m A F#m7
Gtrs. 1 & 2: w/ Rhy. Fill 1
Mes-sage in a bot - tle, yeah.
grad. release
grad. bend
Outro
Gtr. 1: w/ Riff A (till fade)
Gtr. 3 tacet
Gtr. 2: w/ Riff A1 (till fade)
C#sus2 Asus2 Bsus2 F#sus2
Send - ing out an S. O. S.
Send - ing out an S. O. S. I'm send - ing out an S. O. S. I'm
send - ing out an S. O. S. I'm send - ing out an S. O. S.
Send - ing out an S. O. S.
Voc. Fig. 1
End Voc. Fig. 1
Send - ing out an S. O. S.
w/ Voc. Fig. 1 (till fade)
Gtr. 3
8va
loco
mf
rake

# Peace of Mind
### Words and Music by Tom Scholz

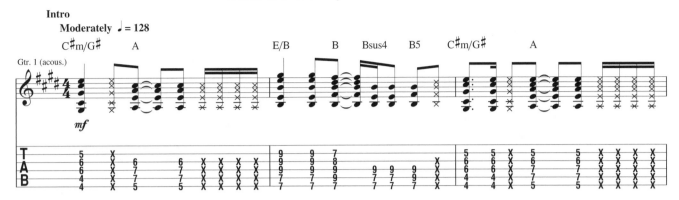

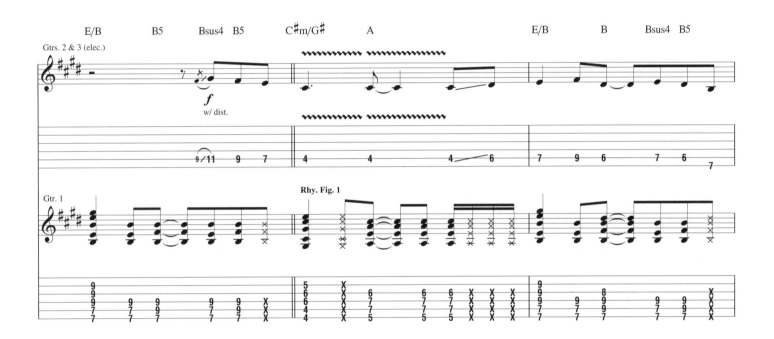

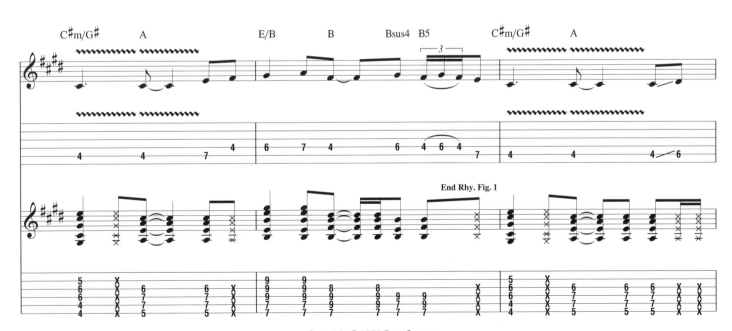

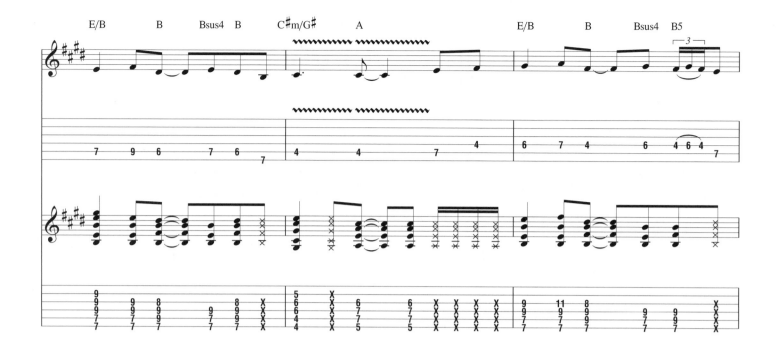

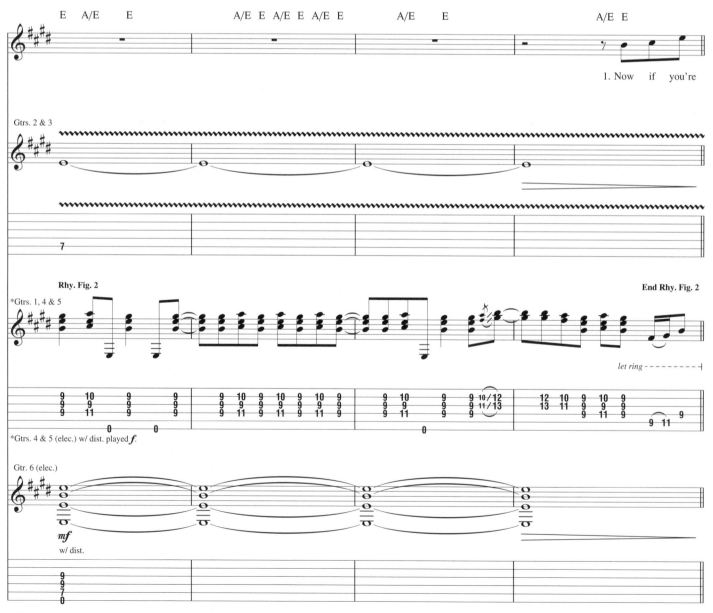

**Verse**

feel - in' kind - a low 'bout the dues you've been pay - ing, fu - ture's com - in' much too slow. —

And you wan - na run but some - how you just keep on stay - in',

can't de - cide on which way to go, _____ whoa. __ Yeah, yeah, yeah.

188

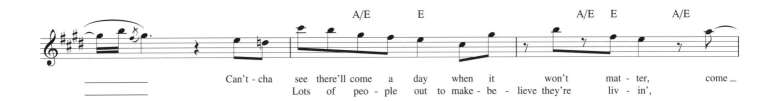

Can't-cha see there'll come a day when it won't mat - ter, come
Lots of peo - ple out to make - be - lieve they're liv - in',

Gtrs. 1 & 5: w/ Rhy. Fig. 4
Gtr. 4: w/ Rhy. Fig. 4A

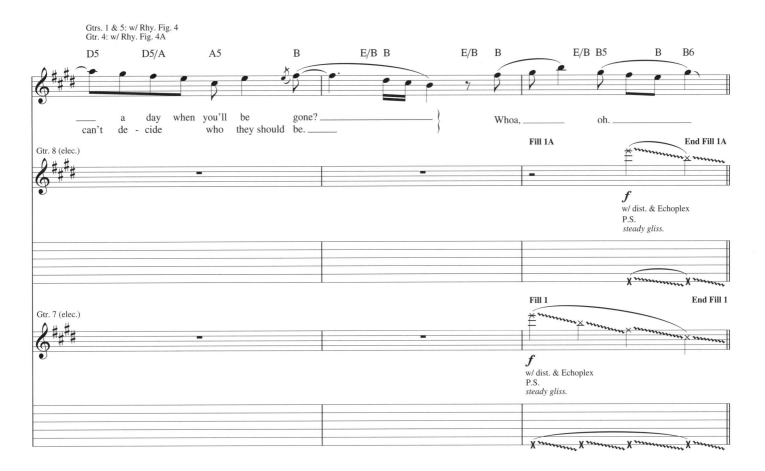

___ a day when you'll be gone? _____
can't de - cide who they should be. ___

Whoa, _____ oh.

Gtr. 8 (elec.)

Fill 1A          End Fill 1A

*f*
w/ dist. & Echoplex
P.S.
*steady gliss.*

Gtr. 7 (elec.)

Fill 1          End Fill 1

*f*
w/ dist. & Echoplex
P.S.
*steady gliss.*

## Chorus

Gtr. 1: w/ Rhy. Fig. 1 (2 times)
Gtrs. 4 & 5: w/ Rhy. Fig. 5 (4 times)
Gtrs. 7 & 8 tacet

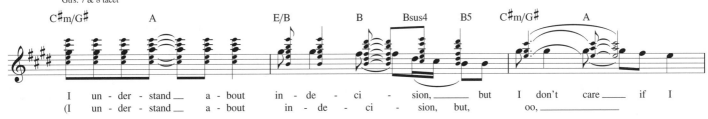

I un - der - stand ___ a - bout in - de - ci - sion, ___ but I don't care ___ if I
(I un - der - stand ___ a - bout in - de - ci - sion, but, oo, _____

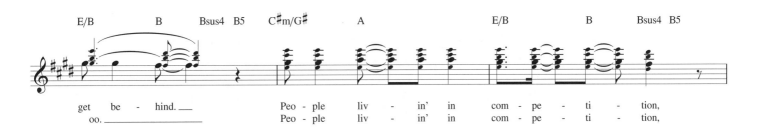

get be - hind. ___          Peo - ple liv - in' in com - pe - ti - tion,
oo.          Peo - ple liv - in' in com - pe - ti - tion,

Gtrs. 1, 4 & 5: w/ Rhy. Fill 1

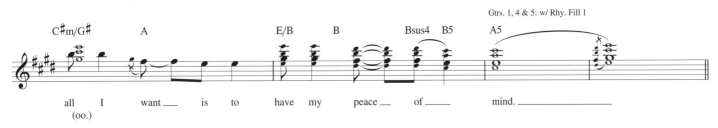

all I want ___ is to have my peace ___ of ___ mind. _____
(oo.)

**Bridge**

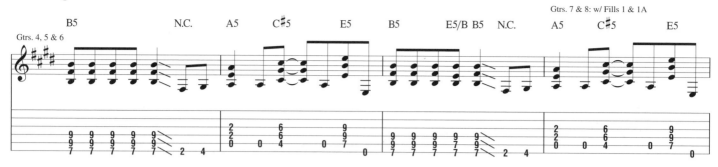

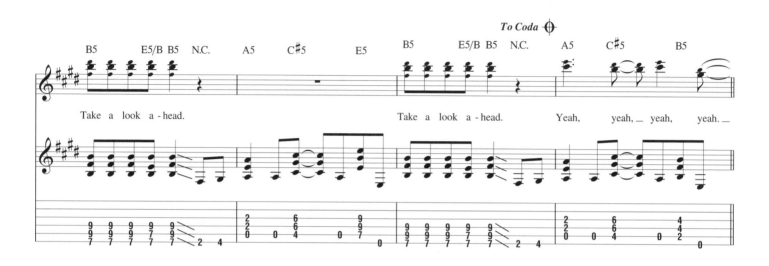

**Interlude**

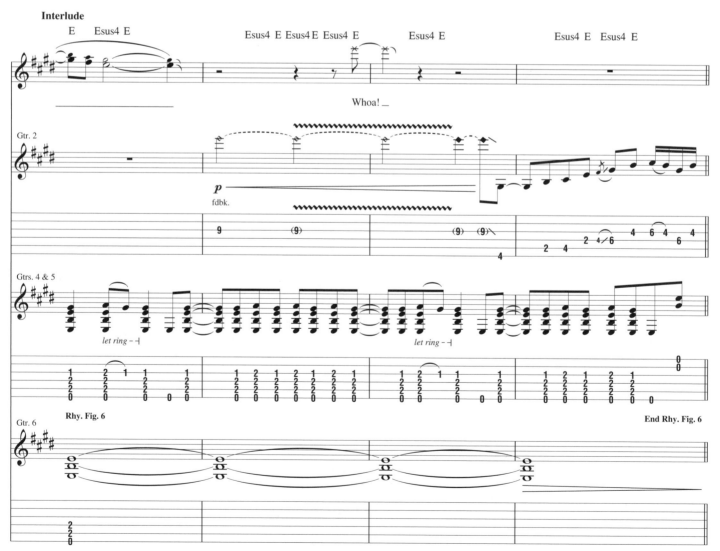

**Guitar Solo**

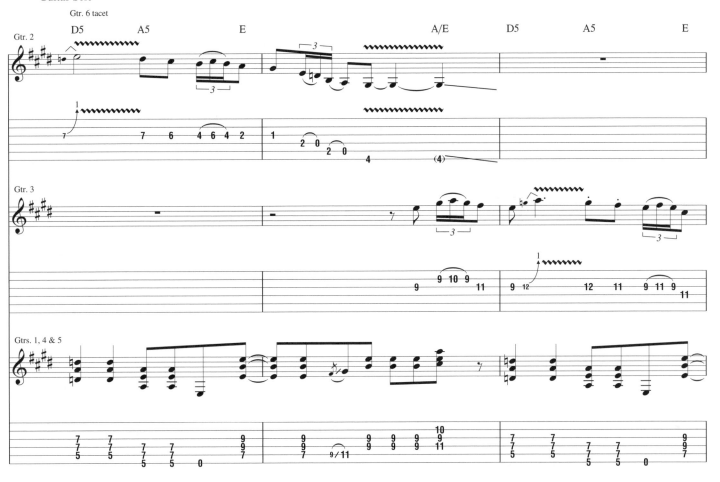

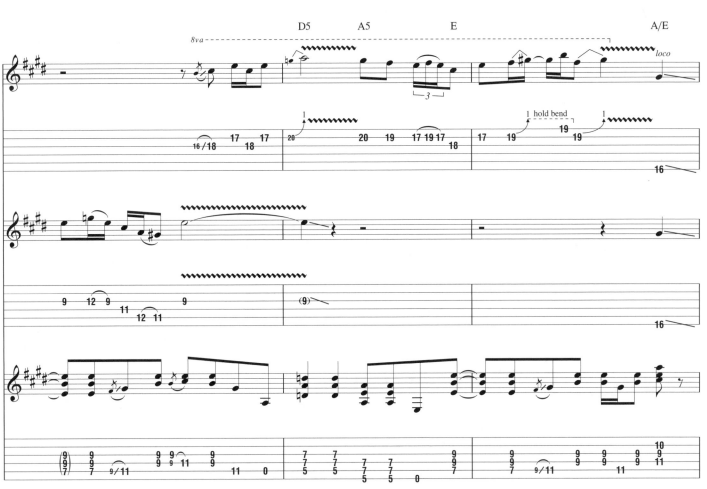

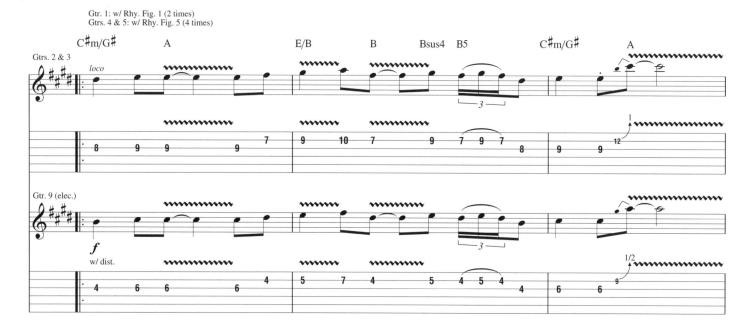

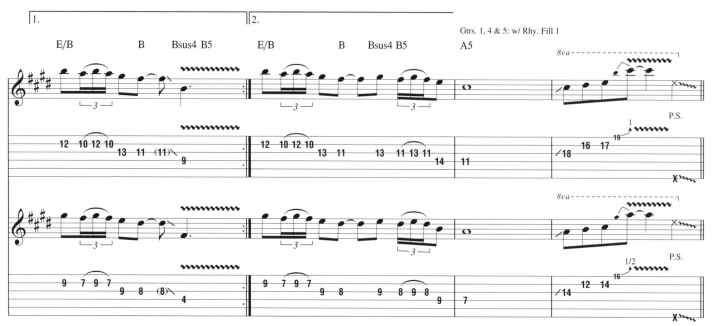

**Interlude**

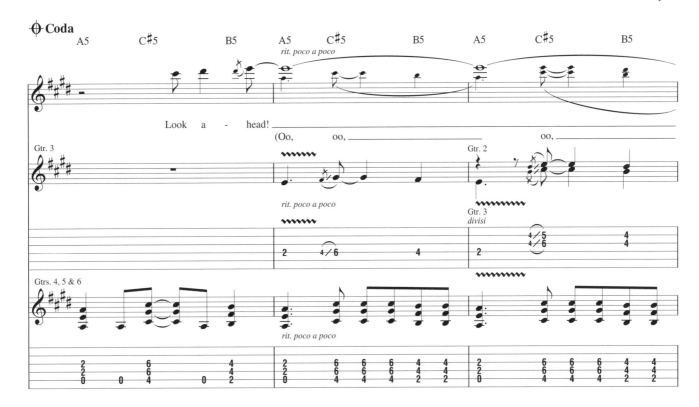

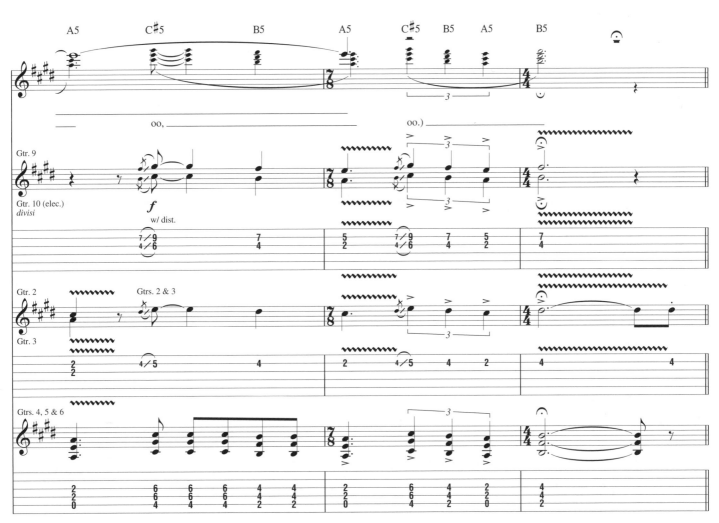

from Steely Dan - *Can't Buy a Thrill*

# Reeling in the Years

## Words and Music by Walter Becker and Donald Fagen

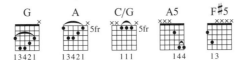

*Chord sumbols reflect implied harmony.

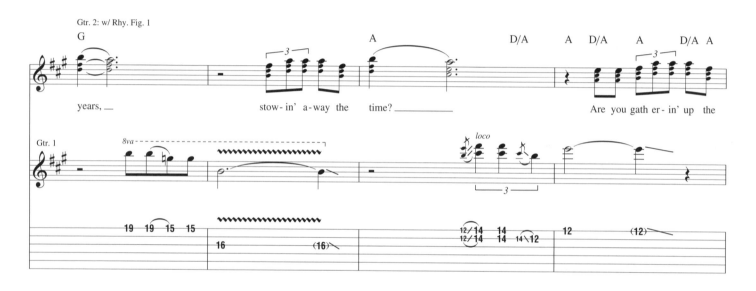

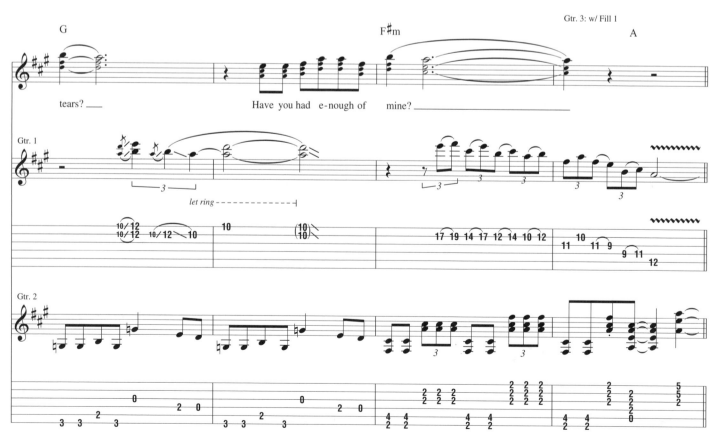

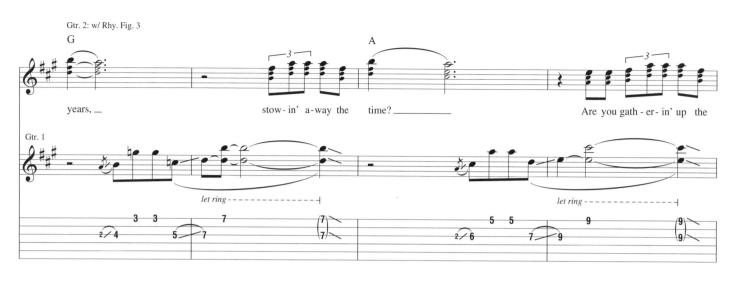

years, ___ stow- in' a-way the time? ___ Are you gath - er- in' up the

tears? ___ Have you had e- nough of mine? ___

**Interlude**

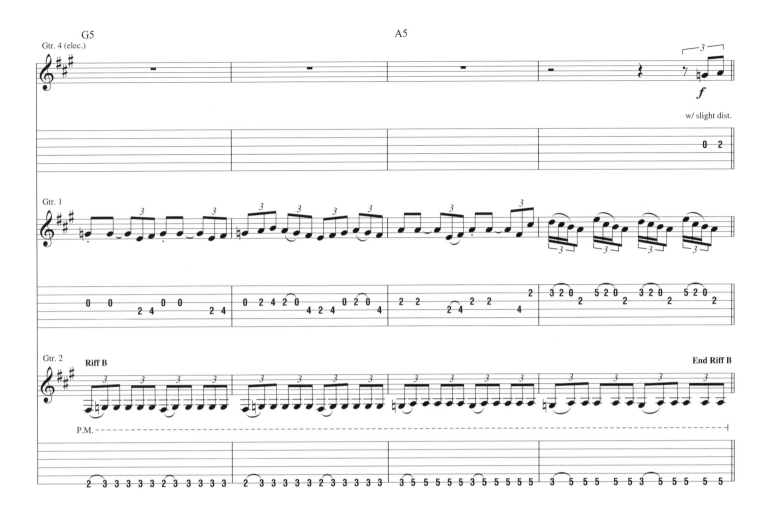

**Guitar Solo** (Elliot Randall)

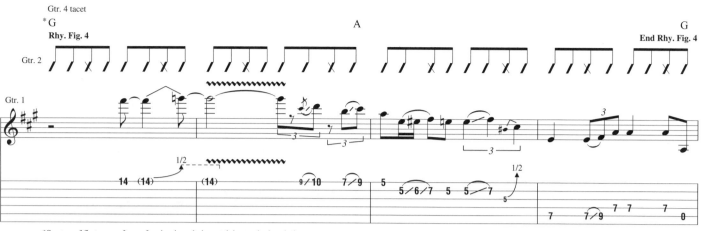

*See top of first page of song for chord symbols pertaining to rhythm slashes.

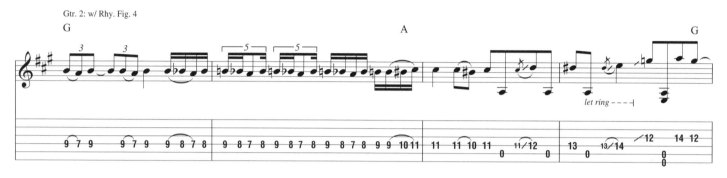

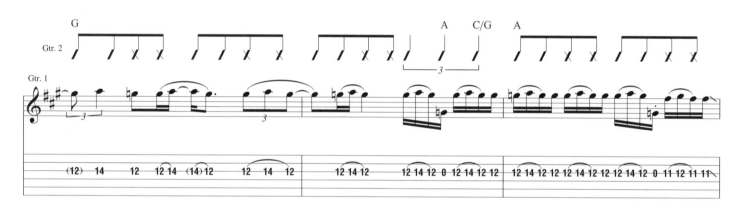

**Verse**

3. I spent a lot of \_\_\_\_ mon - ey and I've spent a lot of time. \_  The trip we made to Hol - ly - wood is etched up -

202

Are you gath-er-in' up the tears? _____ Have you had e-nough of

mine? _____

Gtr. 2: w/ Riff B (2 times)

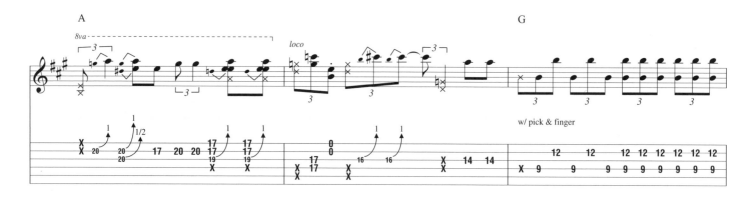

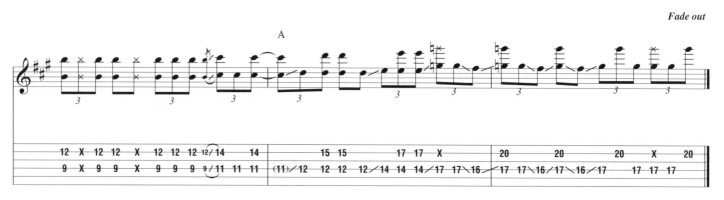

# Refugee

### Words and Music by Tom Petty and Mike Campbell

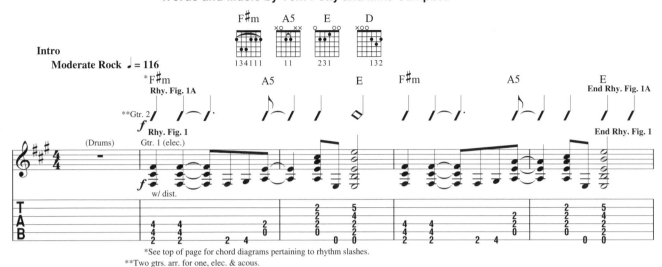

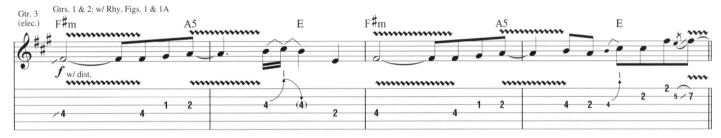

*See top of page for chord diagrams pertaining to rhythm slashes.
**Two gtrs. arr. for one, elec. & acous.

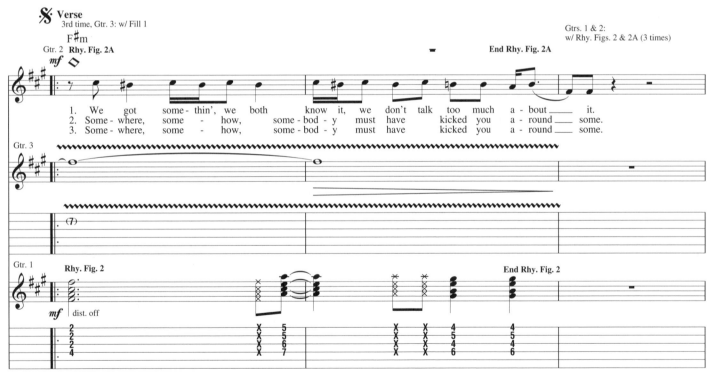

1. We got some-thin', we both know it, we don't talk too much a-bout ____ it.
2. Some-where, some-how, some-bod-y must have kicked you a-round ____ some.
3. Some-where, some-how, some-bod-y must have kicked you a-round ____ some.

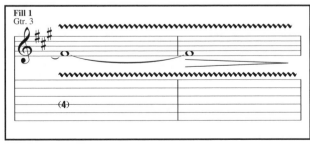

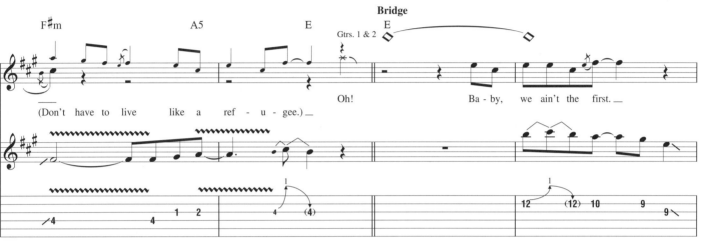

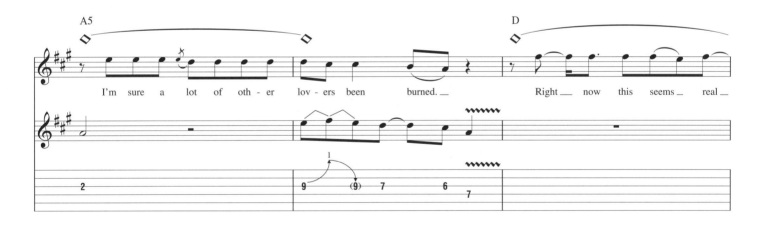

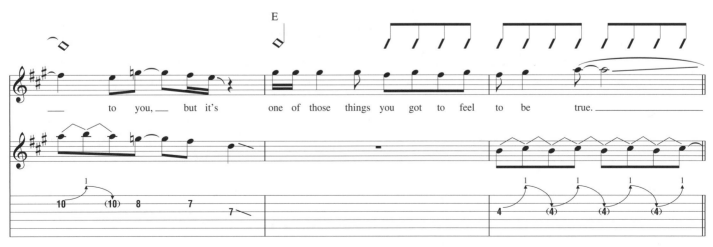

**Organic/Guitar Solo**

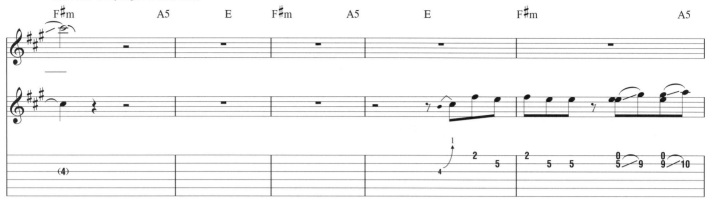

(Don't have to live like a ref - u - gee.) No, you don't have \_\_ to

live like a ref - u - gee. _____ Ba - by, you

Don't have to live like a ref - u - gee. _____

# Rock and Roll Never Forgets

### Words and Music by Bob Seger

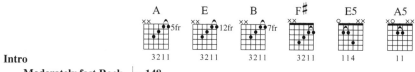

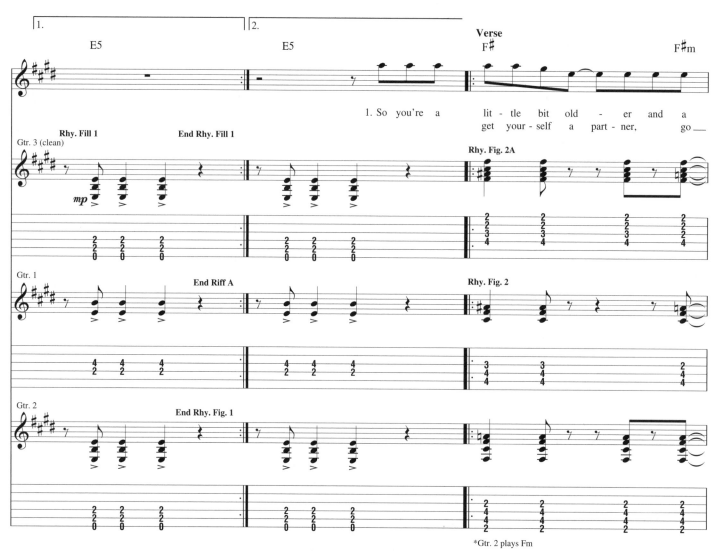

*Chord symbols reflect basic harmony.

*Gtr. 2 plays Fm

dig - ni - ty. _____
_____ too far. _____
So, now
Yeah, the

End Rhy. Fig. 2A

(cont. in slashes)

P.M. - - - - - - - - - - - - - - - - - - - - - - - - -

End Rhy. Fig. 2

P.M. - - - -

𝄋 **Pre-Chorus**

A                          E                          A

Rhy. Fig. 3

Gtr. 3

sweet    six - teen's    turned    thir - ty - one, _____    you
raf - ters    will    be    ring - ing    'cause the    beat's    so    strong, _____    the
sweet    six - teen's    turned    thir - ty - one, _____    the

Gtr. 1

P.M. - - - - - - - - - - - - - - - - - - - - - - - - - - - - - - - - - - -

Gtr. 2

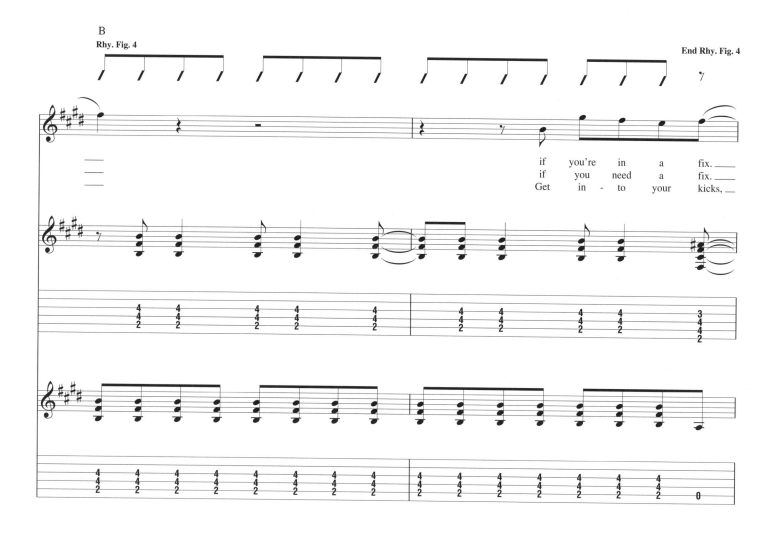

**Guitar Solo**
Gtrs. 1 & 3: w/ Rhy. Figs. 2 & 2A

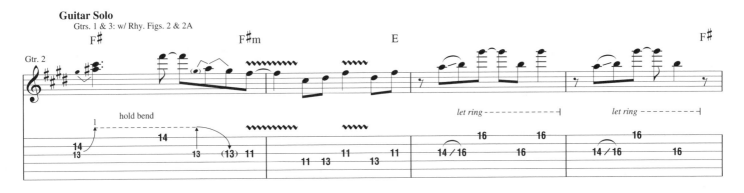

*D.S. al Coda*

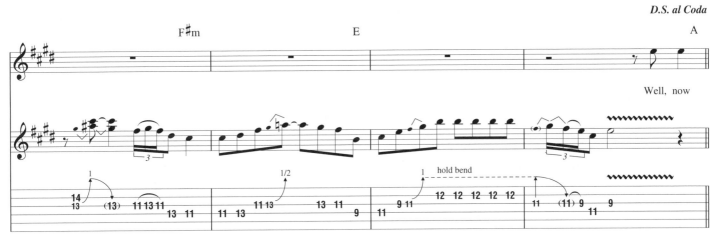

**⊕ Coda**

Gtrs. 1, 2 & 3: w/ Rhy. Figs. 5, 5A & 5B (1st 3 meas.)

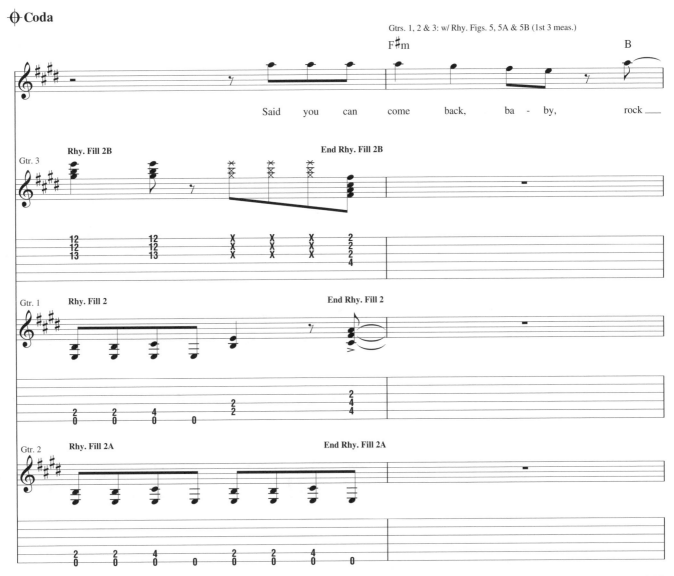

Said you can come back, ba - by, rock ___

## Interlude

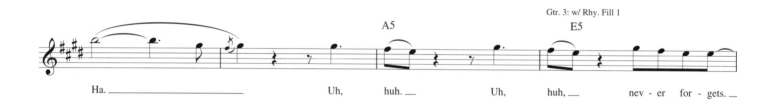

Gtrs. 1, 2 & 3: w/ Rhy. Figs. 6, 6A & 6B

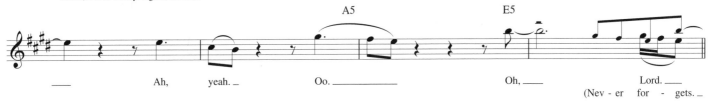

**Outro-Guitar Solo**

Gtrs. 1 & 3: w/ Rhy. Figs. 6 & 6B (till fade)

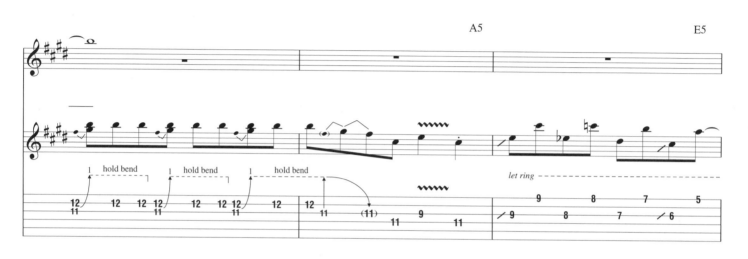

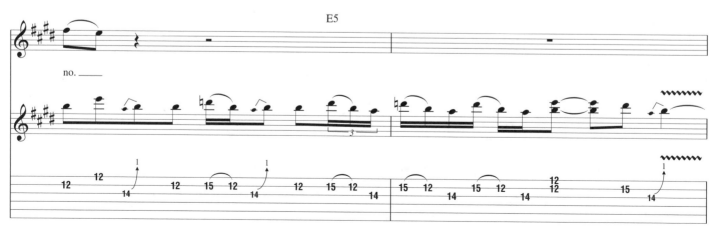

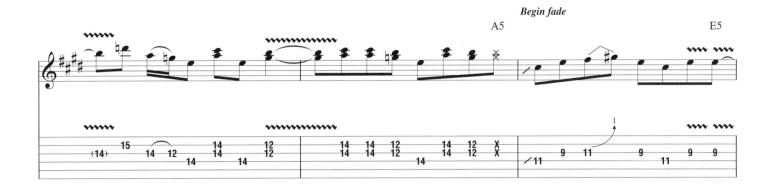

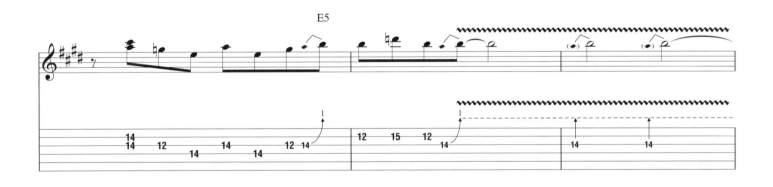

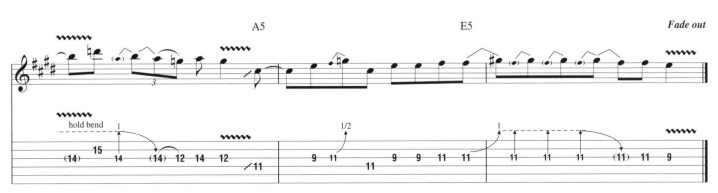

from Yes - *Fragile*

# Roundabout

**Words and Music by Jon Anderson and Steve Howe**

morn-ing driv-ing through the sound and    in and out the   val - ley.

Woo, woo, woo, yeah. Twen - ty-four be - fore, my love, you'll —

— see, I'll __ be there _ with you. ___

*w/ pick & fingers*

**Interlude**
Gtr. 7 tacet

Gtr. 8 (elec.)

*w/ slight dist.*

Gtr. 8 tacet
Em

**Riff D**
Gtr. 9 (elec.)

**End Riff D**

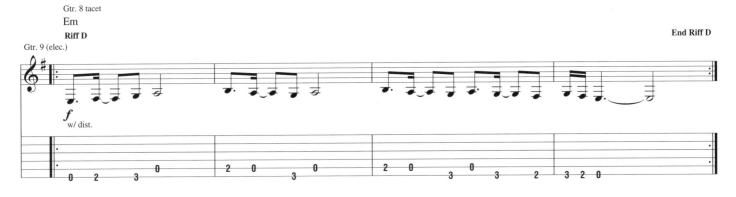

*w/ dist.*

**Bridge**
Gtr. 9: w/ Riff D (3 times)
Em

A - long the drift - ing cloud, _ the ea - gle search - ing down _ on __ the land.

Catch - ing the swirl - ing wind, _ the sail - or sees the rim __ of __ the land.

The ea-gle's danc-ing wings ___ cre-ate as weath-er spins ___ out ___ of hand.

Gtr. 8: w/ Riff D (2 times)

Gtr. 9: w/ Riff D (4 1/2 times)

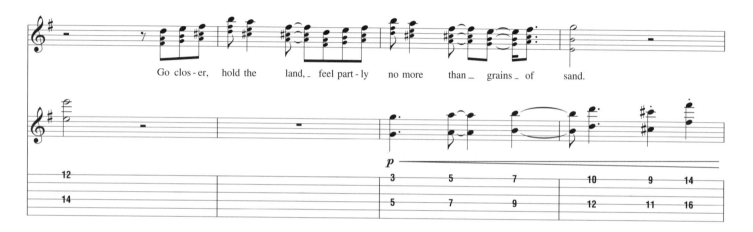

Go clos-er, hold the land, ___ feel part-ly no more than ___ grains ___ of sand.

We stand to lose all time, ___ a thou-sand an-swers by ___ in ___ our hand.

Next to your deep-er fears, ___ we stand sur-round-ed by ___ mil-lion years.

Gtr. 7: w/ Riff E (1 1/2 times)

I'll be the round - a - bout. The words will make

you out and out. I'll be the round - a - bout.

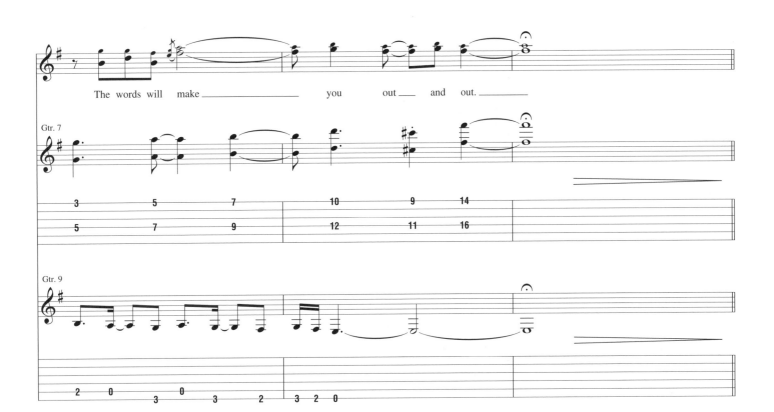

The words will make you out and out.

Gtr. 7

Gtr. 9

## Interlude
### Free time

Gtrs. 7 & 9 tacet

Em

Gtr. 2

Harm.

Harm.

C

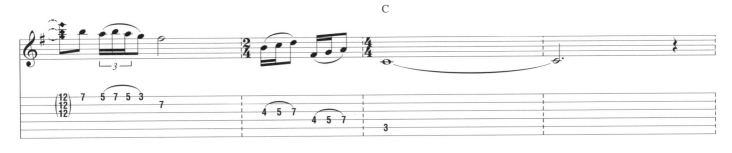

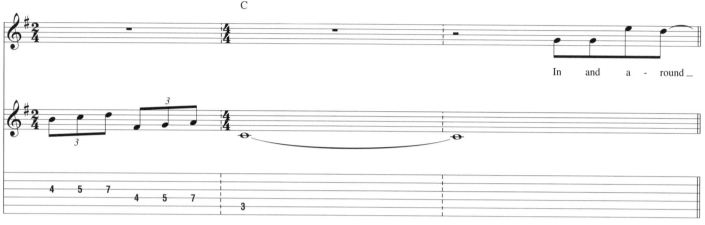

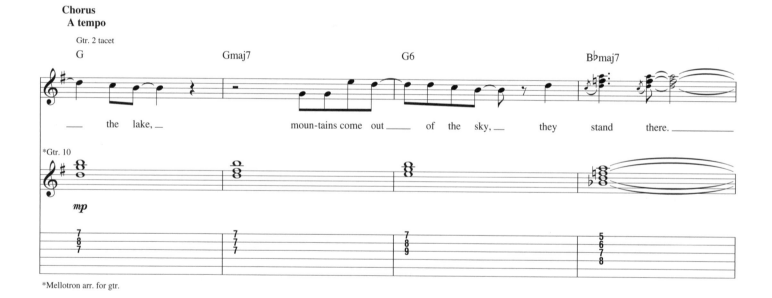

236

**Organic solo**

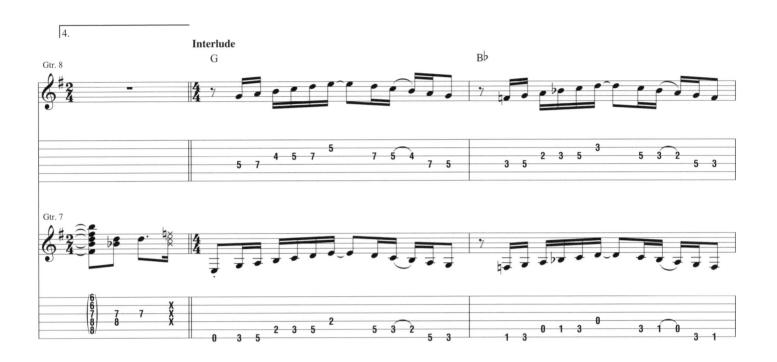

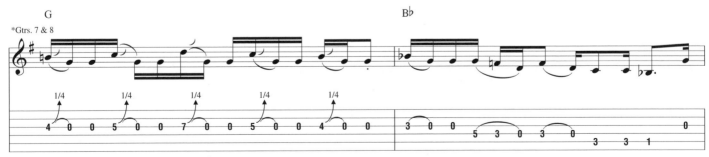

*Composite arrangement

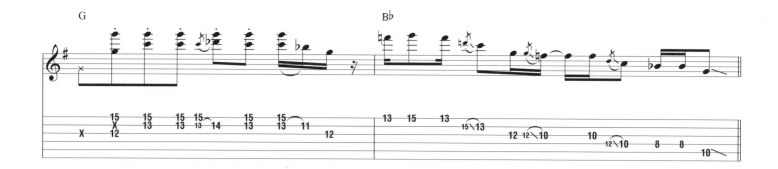

**Organetto solo**

Gtr. 7: w/ Rhy. Fig. 3 (2 times)
Gtr. 8 tacet

**Interlude**

morn-ing driv-ing through the sound and    in and out the    val - ley. _____    In and a - round_

**Chorus**

the lake, _    moun-tains come out _____ of the sky ___ and they stand _____ there. _____

One _____ mile o - ver we'll be there and    we'll see ___ you. _

___    Ten _____ true sum-mers will be there and    laugh - ing, ___ too. _

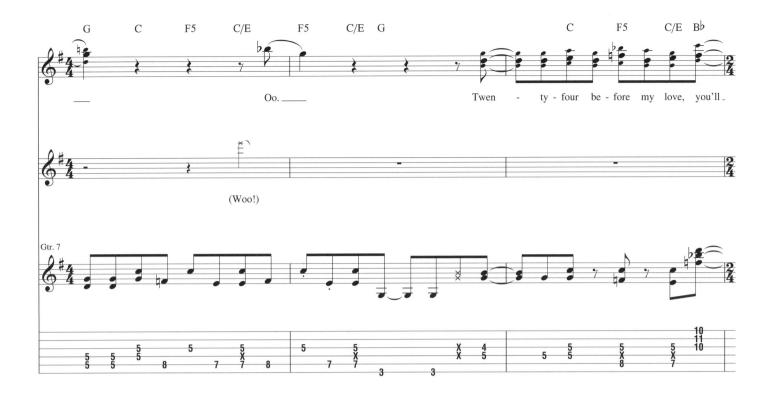

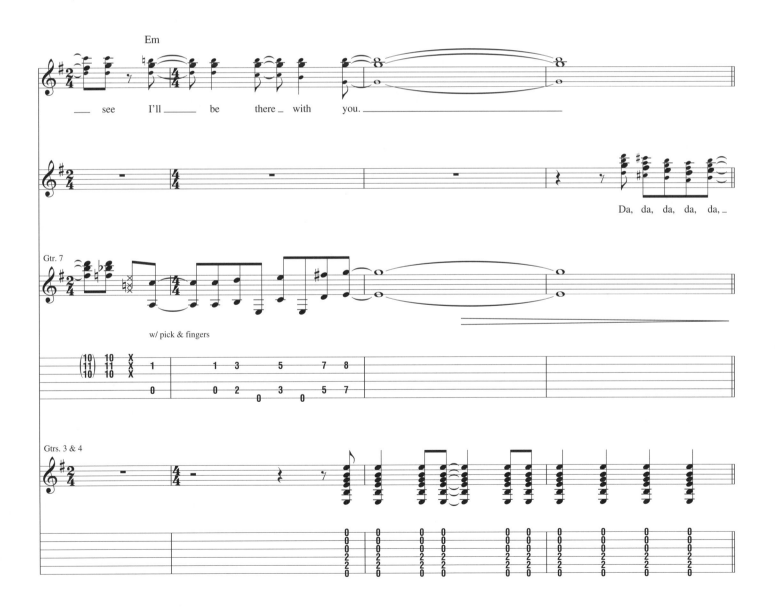

**Outro**

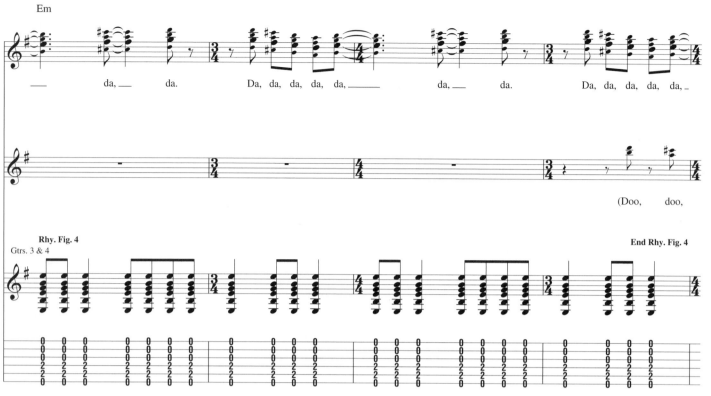

from Rush - *Moving Pictures*

# Tom Sawyer

**Words by Pye Dubois and Neil Peart**
**Music by Geddy Lee and Alex Lifeson**

**Intro**
**Moderately slow** ♩ = 88

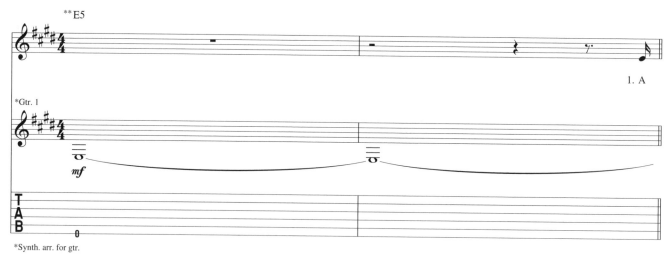

*Synth. arr. for gtr.

**Chord symbols reflect implied harmony.

**Verse**

mod-ern day war-ri-or, \_\_ mean, mean stride. To-day's Tom Saw-yer, mean, \_ mean \_\_ pride.

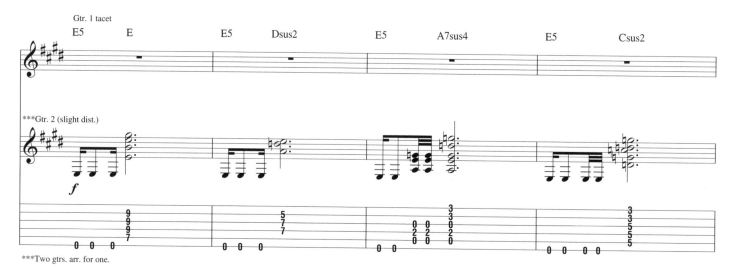

***Gtr. 2 (slight dist.)

***Two gtrs. arr. for one.

Though his mind is not __ for rent, don't put him down as ar - ro-gant. His re - serve, a qui - et de-fense. __

__ Rid - ing out the day's __ e - vents, the __ riv - er.

𝄋 **Interlude**

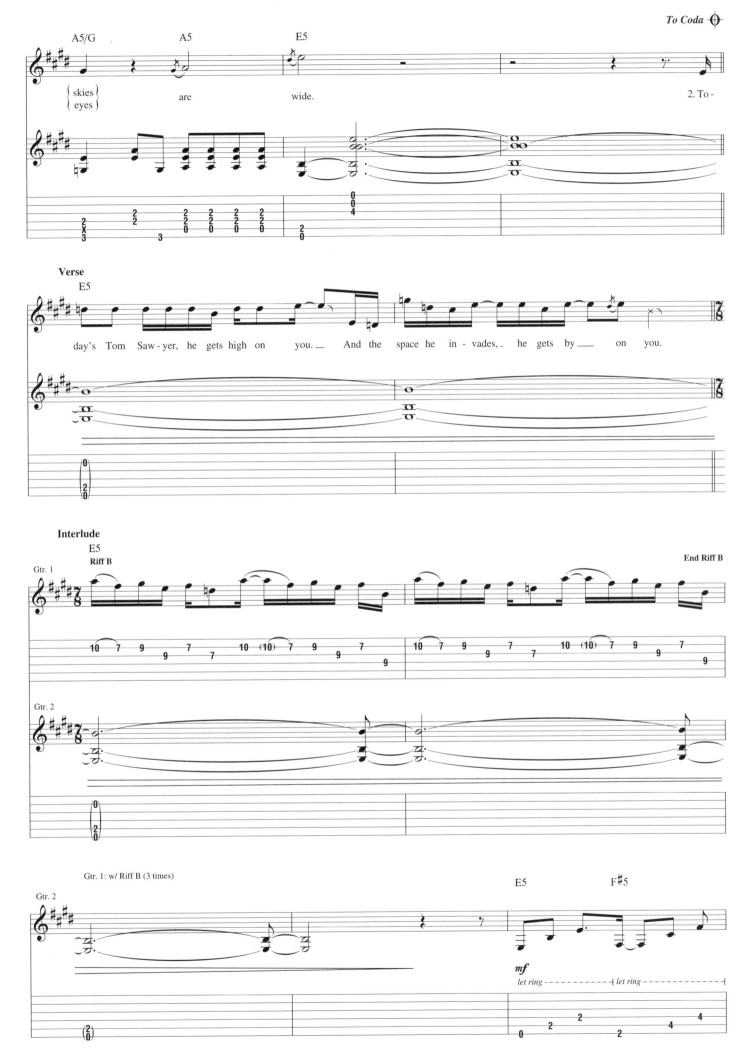

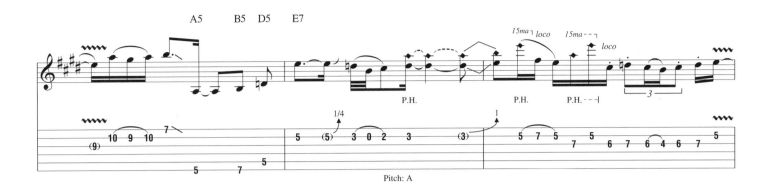

Pitch: A

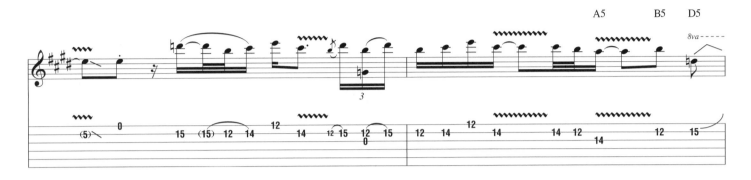

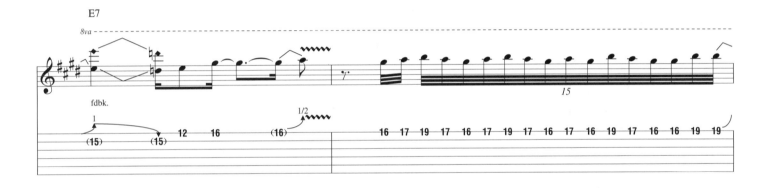

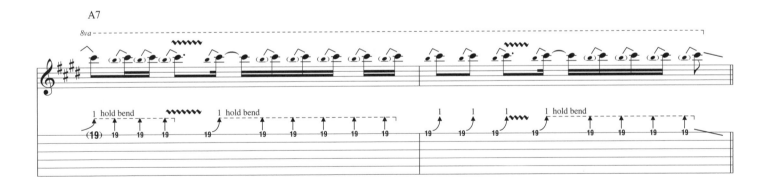

**Interlude**

Gtr. 3 tacet

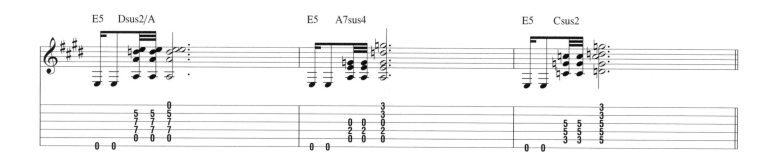

**Verse**

Gtr. 2: w/ Rhy. Fig. 1

E5          E                                    E5          D

3. No, his mind is not___ for rent          to an - y god or gov - ern - ment.

*D.S. al Coda*

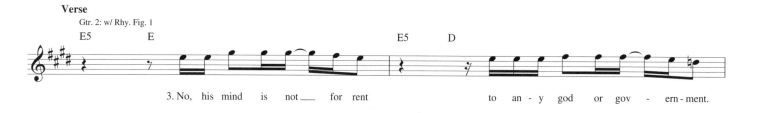

E5 A7sus4                      E5 Csus2                      G/B A7sus4  Csus2 G/B  A7sus4

Al-ways hope-ful, yet dis - con-tent.    He knows chang - es aren't per - ma - nent, ___    but  change _ is.

**⌖ Coda**

**Verse**

E5

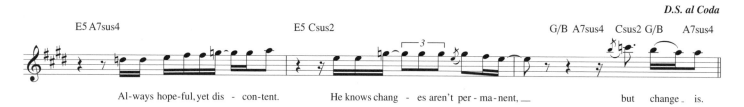

4. Ex - it     the war - ri - or, to-day's Tom Saw-yer. He gets  high on    you ___ and the en - er - gy you      trade. He gets

Gtr. 2

*mp*

fdbk.

Pitch: A

E5                          F#5

right    on       to  the  fric - tion  of  the       day.

*f*

let ring - - - - - - - - - -   let ring - - - - - - - - - - - -

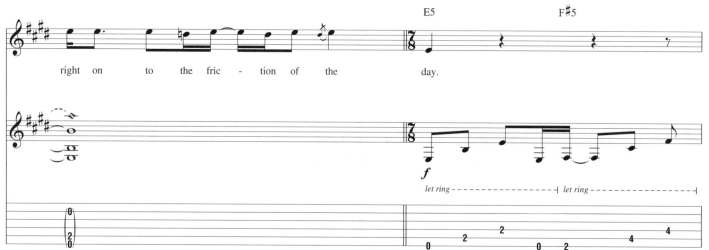

Play 3 times & fade

# Up on Cripple Creek

## Words and Music by Robbie Robertson

*Chord symbols reflect overall harmony.

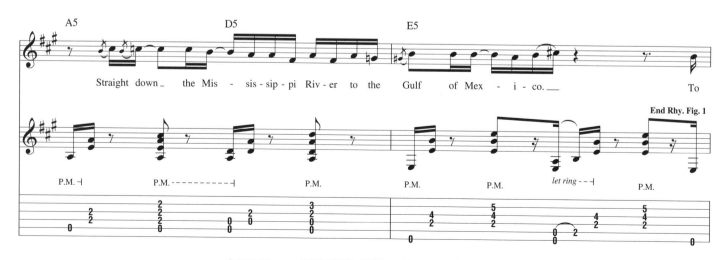

Gtr. 2: w/ Rhy. Fig. 1

Lake Charles, Lou - is - i - an - a, Lit - tle Bes - sie, girl I once knew.

Uh, she told me just to come on by if there's an - y - thing that she could do.

**Chorus**

Up on Crip - ple Creek she sends me. If I spring a leak, she mends me.

Gtr. 2    **Rhy. Fig. 2**

I don't have to speak, uh, she de - fends me. A drunk - ard's dream if I ev - er did see one.

**End Rhy. Fig. 2**

P.M.    *let ring* - - - - - - - - - - - - - - - - - - - - - - - - - - - - - - - -

𝄋 **Verse**

Gtr. 2: w/ Rhy. Fig. 1 (2 times)

2. Good luck had just stung me, to the race track I did go.
took up all of my win - nings and I gave my lit - tle Bes - sie half.
4., 5. *See additional lyrics*

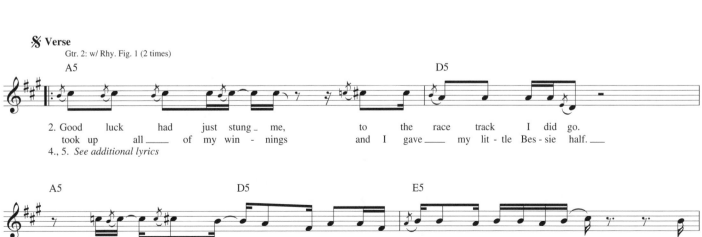

She bet on one horse to win, and I bet on an - oth - er to show.
Uh, she tore it up and threw it in my face, uh, just for a laugh.
Now,

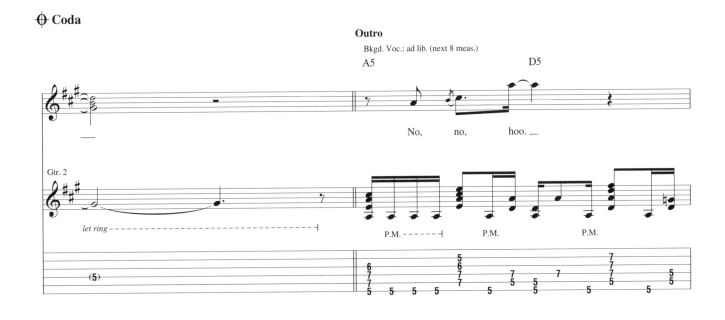

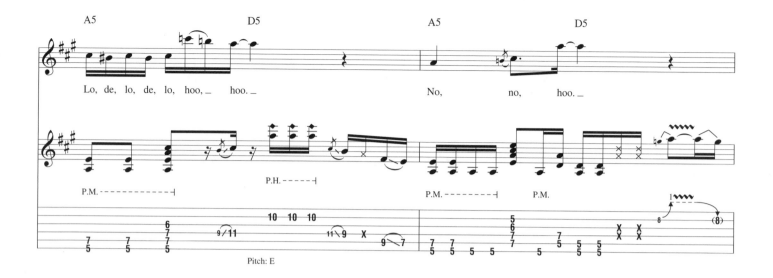

Lo, de, lo, de, lo, hoo, ___ hoo. ___

No, no, hoo. ___

Pitch: E

Lo, de, lo, de, lo, hoo, ___ hoo. ___

Oo, hoo. ___

**Begin fade**

**Fade out**

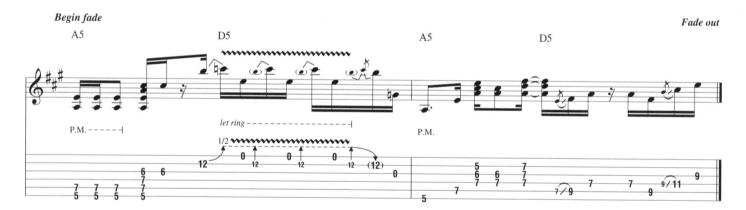

*Additional Lyrics*

4. Now me and my mate were back at the shack,
   We had Spike Jones on the box.
   She said, "I can't take the way he sings
   But I love to hear him talk."
   Now that just gave my heart a throb
   To the bottom of my feet.
   And I swore as I took another pull,
   My Bessie can't be beat.

5. There's a flood out in California,
   And up north it's freezing cold.
   And this livin' off the road
   Is gettin' pretty old.
   So I guess I'll call up my big mama,
   Tell her I'll be rolling in.
   But you know, deep down I'm kinda tempted
   To go and see my Bessie again.

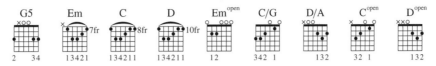

from John Mellencamp - *Dance Naked*

# Wild Night

Words and Music by Van Morrison

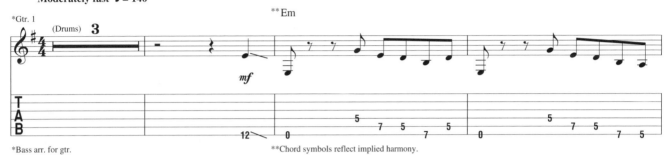

Gtr. 4: Open G tuning:
(low to high) D-G-D-G-B-D

**Intro**
Moderately fast ♩ = 140

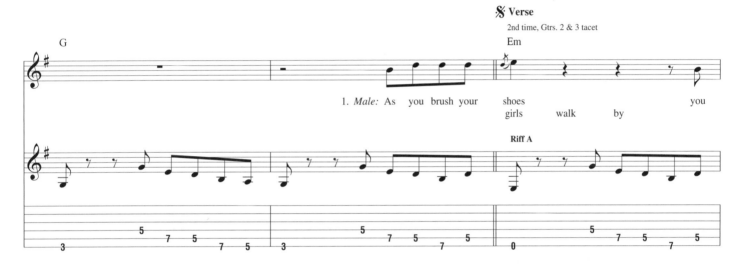

*Bass arr. for gtr.

**Chord symbols reflect implied harmony.

**𝄋 Verse**

2nd time, Gtrs. 2 & 3 tacet

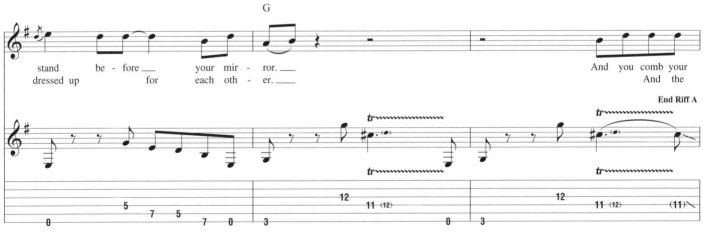

1. *Male:* As you brush your shoes
girls walk by

stand be-fore ___ your mir-ror. ___
dressed up for each oth-er. ___

And you comb your
And the

Gtr. 1: w/ Riff A (2 times)

hair, ___ do the boog-ie woog-ie
boys ___ do the boog-ie woog-ie

grab your coat and hat. ___
on the cor-ner of the street. ___

*Female:* And ___ you walk
*Female:* And the

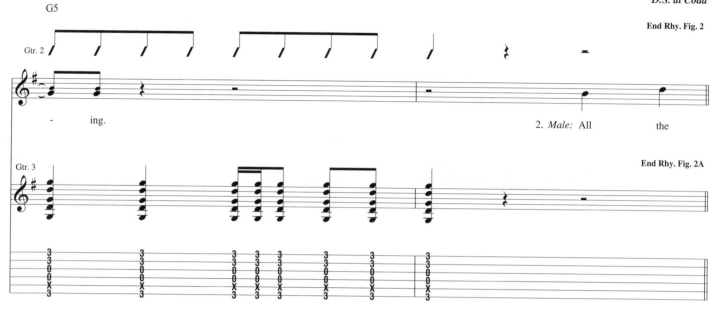

**⊕ Coda**

**Pre-Chorus**

## Chorus

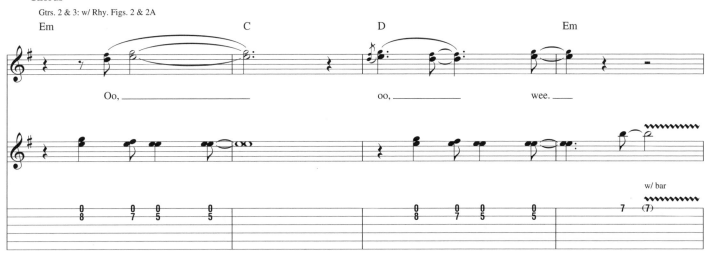

Oo, ___ oo, ___ wee. ___

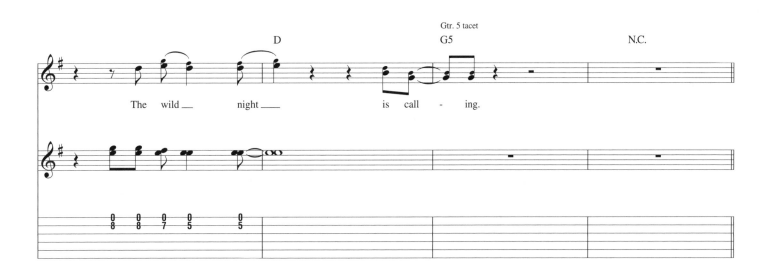

The wild ___ night ___ is call - ing.

## Interlude

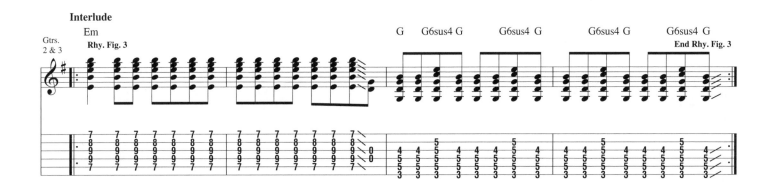

## Guitar Solo

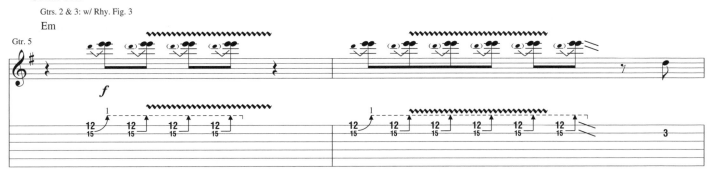

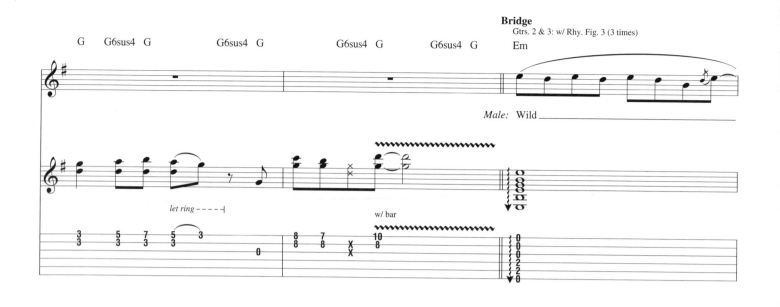

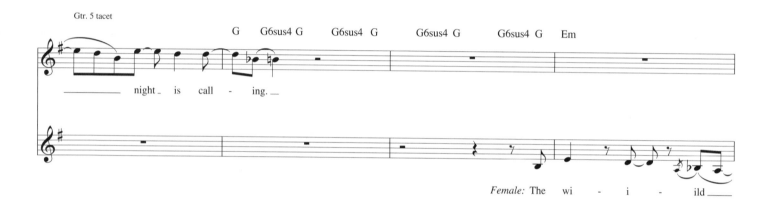

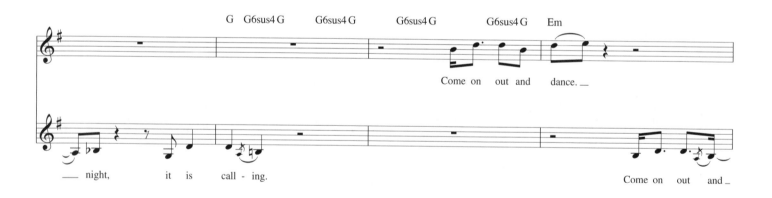

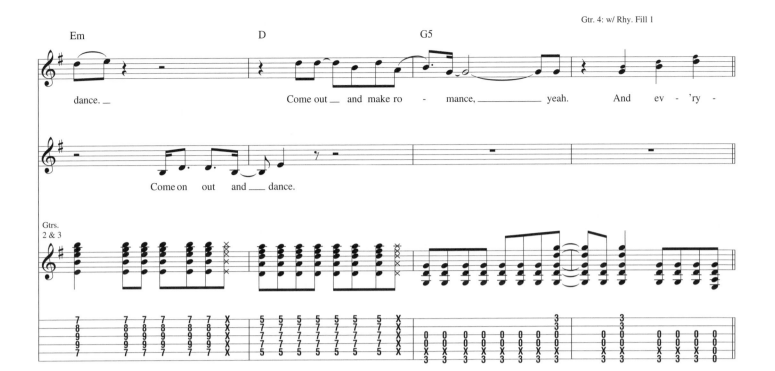

**Pre-Chorus**

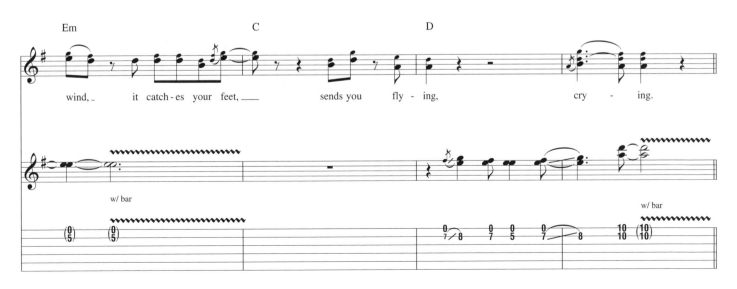

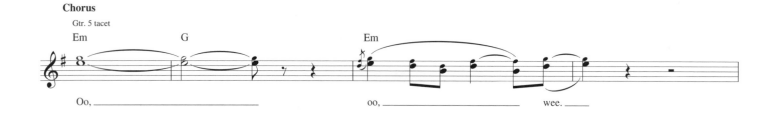

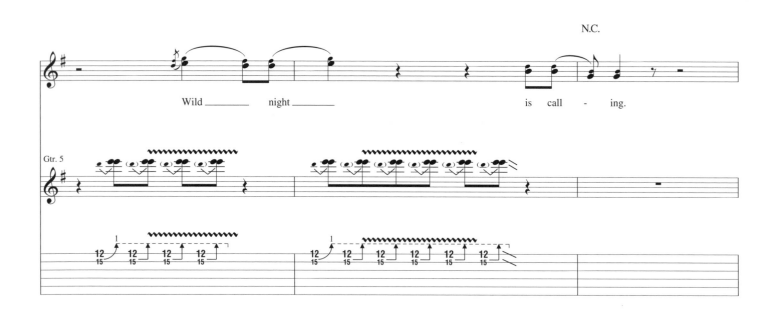

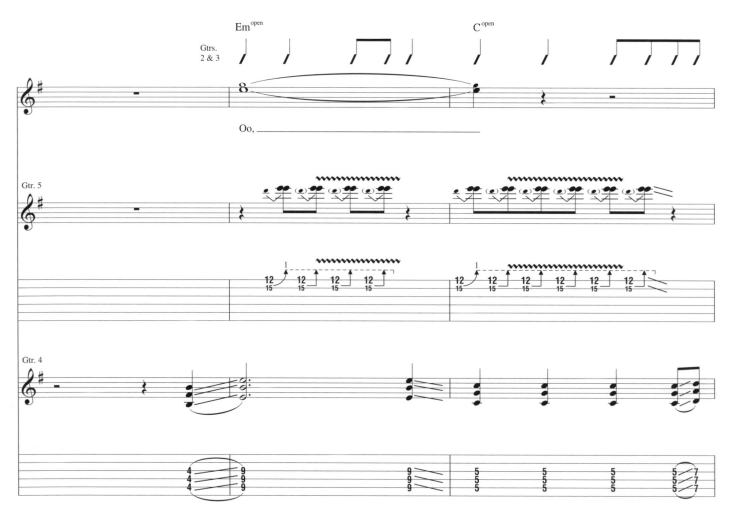

# GUITAR NOTATION LEGEND

Guitar music can be notated three different ways: on a *musical staff*, in *tablature*, and in *rhythm slashes*.

**RHYTHM SLASHES** are written above the staff. Strum chords in the rhythm indicated. Use the chord diagrams found at the top of the first page of the transcription for the appropriate chord voicings. Round noteheads indicate single notes.

**THE MUSICAL STAFF** shows pitches and rhythms and is divided by bar lines into measures. Pitches are named after the first seven letters of the alphabet.

**TABLATURE** graphically represents the guitar fingerboard. Each horizontal line represents a string, and each number represents a fret.

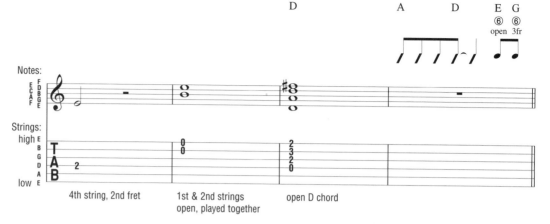

4th string, 2nd fret     1st & 2nd strings open, played together     open D chord

# Definitions for Special Guitar Notation

**HALF-STEP BEND:** Strike the note and bend up 1/2 step.

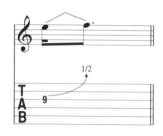

**BEND AND RELEASE:** Strike the note and bend up as indicated, then release back to the original note. Only the first note is struck.

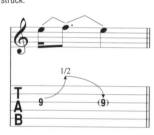

**VIBRATO:** The string is vibrated by rapidly bending and releasing the note with the fretting hand.

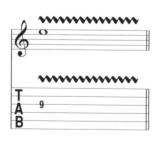

**LEGATO SLIDE:** Strike the first note and then slide the same fret-hand finger up or down to the second note. The second note is not struck.

**WHOLE-STEP BEND:** Strike the note and bend up one step.

**PRE-BEND:** Bend the note as indicated, then strike it.

**WIDE VIBRATO:** The pitch is varied to a greater degree by vibrating with the fretting hand.

**SHIFT SLIDE:** Same as legato slide, except the second note is struck.

**GRACE NOTE BEND:** Strike the note and immediately bend up as indicated.

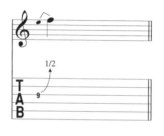

**PRE-BEND AND RELEASE:** Bend the note as indicated. Strike it and release the bend back to the original note.

**HAMMER-ON:** Strike the first (lower) note with one finger, then sound the higher note (on the same string) with another finger by fretting it without picking.

**TRILL:** Very rapidly alternate between the notes indicated by continuously hammering on and pulling off.

**SLIGHT (MICROTONE) BEND:** Strike the note and bend up 1/4 step.

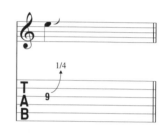

**UNISON BEND:** Strike the two notes simultaneously and bend the lower note up to the pitch of the higher.

**PULL-OFF:** Place both fingers on the notes to be sounded. Strike the first note and without picking, pull the finger off to sound the second (lower) note.

**TAPPING:** Hammer ("tap") the fret indicated with the pick-hand index or middle finger and pull off to the note fretted by the fret hand.

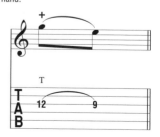

**NATURAL HARMONIC:** Strike the note while the fret-hand lightly touches the string directly over the fret indicated.

**PINCH HARMONIC:** The note is fretted normally and a harmonic is produced by adding the edge of the thumb or the tip of the index finger of the pick hand to the normal pick attack.

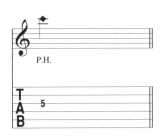

**HARP HARMONIC:** The note is fretted normally and a harmonic is produced by gently resting the pick hand's index finger directly above the indicated fret (in parentheses) while the pick hand's thumb or pick assists by plucking the appropriate string.

**PICK SCRAPE:** The edge of the pick is rubbed down (or up) the string, producing a scratchy sound.

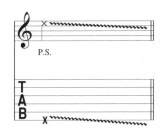

**MUFFLED STRINGS:** A percussive sound is produced by laying the fret hand across the string(s) without depressing, and striking them with the pick hand.

**PALM MUTING:** The note is partially muted by the pick hand lightly touching the string(s) just before the bridge.

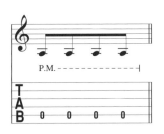

**RAKE:** Drag the pick across the strings indicated with a single motion.

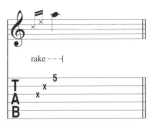

**TREMOLO PICKING:** The note is picked as rapidly and continuously as possible.

**ARPEGGIATE:** Play the notes of the chord indicated by quickly rolling them from bottom to top.

**VIBRATO BAR DIVE AND RETURN:** The pitch of the note or chord is dropped a specified number of steps (in rhythm), then returned to the original pitch.

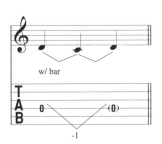

**VIBRATO BAR SCOOP:** Depress the bar just before striking the note, then quickly release the bar.

**VIBRATO BAR DIP:** Strike the note and then immediately drop a specified number of steps, then release back to the original pitch.

# Additional Musical Definitions

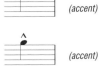 *(accent)* • Accentuate note (play it louder).

 *(accent)* • Accentuate note with great intensity.

*(staccato)* • Play the note short.

• Downstroke

∨ • Upstroke

***D.S. al Coda*** • Go back to the sign (𝄋), then play until the measure marked "***To Coda***," then skip to the section labelled "**Coda**."

***D.C. al Fine*** • Go back to the beginning of the song and play until the measure marked "***Fine***" (end).

**Rhy. Fig.** • Label used to recall a recurring accompaniment pattern (usually chordal).

**Riff** • Label used to recall composed, melodic lines (usually single notes) which recur.

**Fill** • Label used to identify a brief melodic figure which is to be inserted into the arrangement.

**Rhy. Fill** • A chordal version of a Fill.

tacet • Instrument is silent (drops out).

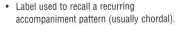 • Repeat measures between signs.

 • When a repeated section has different endings, play the first ending only the first time and the second ending only the second time.

**NOTE:** Tablature numbers in parentheses mean:
    1. The note is being sustained over a system (note in standard notation is tied), or
    2. The note is sustained, but a new articulation (such as a hammer-on, pull-off, slide or vibrato) begins, or
    3. The note is a barely audible "ghost" note (note in standard notation is also in parentheses).

# GUITAR RECORDED VERSIONS®

*Guitar Recorded Versions® are note-for-note transcriptions of guitar music taken directly off recordings*
*This series, one of the most popular in print today, features some of the greatest*
*guitar players and groups from blues and rock to country and jazz.*

*Guitar Recorded Versions are transcribed by the best transcribers in the business*
*Every book contains notes and tablature. Visit **www.balleonard.com** for our complete selection.*

**AUTHENTIC TRANSCRIPTIONS**
**WITH NOTES AND TABLATURE**

| | | |
|---|---|---|
| 00690898 | John 5 – The Devil Knows My Name | $22.95 |
| 00690959 | John 5 – Requiem | $22.95 |
| 00690814 | John 5 – Songs for Sanity | $19.95 |
| 00690751 | John 5 – Vertigo | $19.95 |
| 00694912 | Eric Johnson – Ah Via Musicom | $19.95 |
| 00690660 | Best of Eric Johnson | $22.99 |
| 00690845 | Eric Johnson – Bloom | $19.95 |
| 00691076 | Eric Johnson – Up Close | $22.99 |
| 00690169 | Eric Johnson – Venus Isle | $22.95 |
| 00690846 | Jack Johnson and Friends – Sing-A-Longs and Lullabies for the Film Curious George | $19.95 |
| 00690271 | Robert Johnson – The New Transcriptions | $24.95 |
| 00699131 | Best of Janis Joplin | $19.95 |
| 00690427 | Best of Judas Priest | $22.99 |
| 00690651 | Juanes – Exitos de Juanes | $19.95 |
| 00690277 | Best of Kansas | $19.95 |
| 00690911 | Best of Phil Keaggy | $24.99 |
| 00690727 | Toby Keith Guitar Collection | $19.99 |
| 00690888 | The Killers – Sam's Town | $19.95 |
| 00690504 | Very Best of Albert King | $19.95 |
| 00690444 | B.B. King & Eric Clapton – Riding with the King | $22.99 |
| 00690134 | Freddie King Collection | $19.95 |
| 00691062 | Kings of Leon – Come Around Sundown | $22.99 |
| 00690975 | Kings of Leon – Only by the Night | $22.99 |
| 00690339 | Best of the Kinks | $19.95 |
| 00690157 | Kiss – Alive! | $19.95 |
| 00690356 | Kiss – Alive II | $22.99 |
| 00694903 | Best of Kiss for Guitar | $24.95 |
| 00690355 | Kiss – Destroyer | $16.95 |
| 14026320 | Mark Knopfler – Get Lucky | $22.99 |
| 00690164 | Mark Knopfler Guitar – Vol. 1 | $19.95 |
| 00690163 | Mark Knopfler/Chet Atkins – Neck and Neck | $19.95 |
| 00690780 | Korn – Greatest Hits, Volume 1 | $22.95 |
| 00690836 | Korn – See You on the Other Side | $19.95 |
| 00690377 | Kris Kristofferson Collection | $19.95 |
| 00690861 | Kutless – Hearts of the Innocent | $19.95 |
| 00690834 | Lamb of God – Ashes of the Wake | $19.95 |
| 00690875 | Lamb of God – Sacrament | $19.95 |
| 00690977 | Ray LaMontagne – Gossip in the Grain | $19.99 |
| 00690890 | Ray LaMontagne – Till the Sun Turns Black | $19.95 |
| 00690823 | Ray LaMontagne – Trouble | $19.95 |
| 00691057 | Ray LaMontagne and the Pariah Dogs – God Willin' & The Creek Don't Rise | $22.99 |
| 00690658 | Johnny Lang – Long Time Coming | $19.95 |
| 00690679 | John Lennon – Guitar Collection | $19.95 |
| 00690781 | Linkin Park – Hybrid Theory | $22.95 |
| 00690782 | Linkin Park – Meteora | $22.95 |
| 00690922 | Linkin Park – Minutes to Midnight | $19.95 |
| 00690783 | Best of Live | $19.95 |
| 00699623 | The Best of Chuck Loeb | $19.95 |
| 00690743 | Los Lonely Boys | $19.95 |
| 00690720 | Lostprophets – Start Something | $19.95 |
| 00690525 | Best of George Lynch | $24.99 |
| 00690955 | Lynyrd Skynyrd – All-Time Greatest Hits | $19.99 |
| 00694954 | New Best of Lynyrd Skynyrd | $19.95 |
| 00690577 | Yngwie Malmsteen – Anthology | $24.95 |
| 00694845 | Yngwie Malmsteen – Fire and Ice | $19.95 |
| 00694757 | Yngwie Malmsteen – Trilogy | $19.95 |
| 00690754 | Marilyn Manson – Lest We Forget | $19.95 |
| 00694956 | Bob Marley – Legend | $19.95 |
| 00690548 | Very Best of Bob Marley & The Wailers – One Love | $22.99 |
| 00694945 | Bob Marley – Songs of Freedom | $24.95 |
| 00690914 | Maroon 5 – It Won't Be Soon Before Long | $19.95 |
| 00690657 | Maroon 5 – Songs About Jane | $19.95 |
| 00690748 | Maroon 5 – 1.22.03 Acoustic | $19.95 |
| 00690989 | Mastodon – Crack the Skye | $22.99 |
| 00691176 | Mastodon – The Hunter | $22.99 |
| 00690442 | Matchbox 20 – Mad Season | $19.95 |
| 00690616 | Matchbox Twenty – More Than You Think You Are | $19.95 |
| 00690239 | Matchbox 20 – Yourself or Someone like You | $19.95 |
| 00691034 | Andy McKee – Joyland | $19.99 |
| 00690382 | Sarah McLachlan – Mirrorball | $19.95 |
| 00120080 | The Don McLean Songbook | $19.95 |
| 00694952 | Megadeth – Countdown to Extinction | $22.95 |
| 00690244 | Megadeth – Cryptic Writings | $19.95 |
| 00694951 | Megadeth – Rust in Peace | $22.95 |
| 00690011 | Megadeth – Youthanasia | $19.95 |
| 00690505 | John Mellencamp Guitar Collection | $19.95 |
| 00690562 | Pat Metheny – Bright Size Life | $19.95 |
| 00691073 | Pat Metheny with Christian McBride & Antonion Sanchez – Day Trip/Tokyo Day Trip Live | $22.99 |
| 00690646 | Pat Metheny – One Quiet Night | $19.95 |
| 00690559 | Pat Metheny – Question & Answer | $19.95 |
| 00690040 | Steve Miller Band Greatest Hits | $19.95 |
| 00690769 | Modest Mouse – Good News for People Who Love Bad News | $19.95 |
| 00102591 | Wes Montgomery Guitar Anthology | $24.99 |
| 00694802 | Gary Moore – Still Got the Blues | $22.99 |
| 00691005 | Best of Motion City Soundtrack | $19.99 |
| 00690787 | Mudvayne – L.D. 50 | $22.95 |
| 00691070 | Mumford & Sons – Sigh No More | $22.99 |
| 00690996 | My Morning Jacket Collection | $19.99 |
| 00690984 | Matt Nathanson – Some Mad Hope | $22.99 |
| 00690611 | Nirvana | $22.95 |
| 00694895 | Nirvana – Bleach | $19.95 |
| 00690189 | Nirvana – From the Muddy Banks of the Wishkah | $19.95 |
| 00694913 | Nirvana – In Utero | $19.95 |
| 00694883 | Nirvana – Nevermind | $19.95 |
| 00690026 | Nirvana – Unplugged in New York | $19.95 |
| 00120112 | No Doubt – Tragic Kingdom | $22.95 |
| 00690226 | Oasis – The Other Side of Oasis | $19.95 |
| 00307163 | Oasis – Time Flies... 1994-2009 | $19.99 |
| 00690358 | The Offspring – Americana | $19.95 |
| 00690203 | The Offspring – Smash | $18.95 |
| 00690818 | The Best of Opeth | $22.95 |
| 00691052 | Roy Orbison – Black & White Night | $22.99 |
| 00694847 | Best of Ozzy Osbourne | $22.95 |
| 00690399 | Ozzy Osbourne – The Ozzman Cometh | $22.99 |
| 00690129 | Ozzy Osbourne – Ozzmosis | $22.95 |
| 00690933 | Best of Brad Paisley | $22.95 |
| 00690995 | Brad Paisley – Play: The Guitar Album | $24.99 |
| 00690866 | Panic! At the Disco – A Fever You Can't Sweat Out | $19.95 |
| 00690939 | Christopher Parkening – Solo Pieces | $19.99 |
| 00690594 | Best of Les Paul | $19.95 |
| 00694855 | Pearl Jam – Ten | $22.99 |
| 00690439 | A Perfect Circle – Mer De Noms | $19.95 |
| 00690661 | A Perfect Circle – Thirteenth Step | $19.95 |
| 00690725 | Best of Carl Perkins | $19.99 |
| 00690499 | Tom Petty – Definitive Guitar Collection | $19.95 |
| 00690868 | Tom Petty – Highway Companion | $19.95 |
| 00690176 | Phish – Billy Breathes | $22.95 |
| 00691249 | Phish – Junta | $22.99 |
| 00690428 | Pink Floyd – Dark Side of the Moon | $19.95 |
| 00690789 | Best of Poison | $19.95 |
| 00693864 | Best of The Police | $19.95 |
| 00690299 | Best of Elvis: The King of Rock 'n' Roll | $19.95 |
| 00692535 | Elvis Presley | $19.95 |
| 00690925 | The Very Best of Prince | $22.99 |
| 00690003 | Classic Queen | $24.95 |
| 00694975 | Queen – Greatest Hits | $24.95 |
| 00690670 | Very Best of Queensryche | $19.95 |
| 00690878 | The Raconteurs – Broken Boy Soldiers | $19.95 |
| 00694910 | Rage Against the Machine | $19.95 |
| 00690179 | Rancid – And Out Come the Wolves | $22.95 |
| 00690426 | Best of Ratt | $19.95 |
| 00690055 | Red Hot Chili Peppers – Blood Sugar Sex Magik | $19.95 |
| 00690584 | Red Hot Chili Peppers – By the Way | $19.95 |
| 00690379 | Red Hot Chili Peppers – Californication | $19.95 |
| 00690673 | Red Hot Chili Peppers – Greatest Hits | $19.95 |
| 00690090 | Red Hot Chili Peppers – One Hot Minute | $22.95 |
| 00691166 | Red Hot Chili Peppers – I'm with You | $22.99 |
| 00690852 | Red Hot Chili Peppers – Stadium Arcadium | $24.95 |
| 00690893 | The Red Jumpsuit Apparatus – Don't You Fake It | $19.95 |
| 00690511 | Django Reinhardt – The Definitive Collection | $19.95 |
| 00690779 | Relient K – MMHMM | $19.95 |
| 00690643 | Relient K – Two Lefts Don't Make a Right ... But Three Do | $19.95 |
| 00690260 | Jimmie Rodgers Guitar Collection | $19.95 |
| 14041901 | Rodrigo Y Gabriela and C.U.B.A. – Area 52 | $24.99 |
| 00690014 | Rolling Stones – Exile on Main Street | $24.95 |
| 00690631 | Rolling Stones – Guitar Anthology | $27.95 |
| 00690685 | David Lee Roth – Eat 'Em and Smile | $19.95 |
| 00690031 | Santana's Greatest Hits | $19.95 |
| 00690796 | Very Best of Michael Schenker | $19.95 |
| 00690566 | Best of Scorpions | $22.95 |
| 00690604 | Bob Seger – Guitar Anthology | $19.95 |
| 00690659 | Bob Seger and the Silver Bullet Band – Greatest Hits, Volume 2 | $17.95 |
| 00691012 | Shadows Fall – Retribution | $22.99 |
| 00690896 | Shadows Fall – Threads of Life | $19.95 |
| 00690803 | Best of Kenny Wayne Shepherd Band | $19.95 |
| 00690750 | Kenny Wayne Shepherd – The Place You're In | $19.95 |
| 00690857 | Shinedown – Us and Them | $19.95 |
| 00690196 | Silverchair – Freak Show | $19.95 |
| 00690130 | Silverchair – Frogstomp | $19.95 |
| 00690872 | Slayer – Christ Illusion | $19.95 |
| 00690813 | Slayer – Guitar Collection | $19.95 |
| 00690419 | Slipknot | $19.95 |
| 00690973 | Slipknot – All Hope Is Gone | $22.99 |
| 00690733 | Slipknot – Volume 3 (The Subliminal Verses) | $22.99 |
| 00690330 | Social Distortion – Live at the Roxy | $19.95 |
| 00120004 | Best of Steely Dan | $24.95 |
| 00694921 | Best of Steppenwolf | $22.95 |
| 00690655 | Best of Mike Stern | $19.95 |

RECORDED VERSIONS GUITAR®

**AUTHENTIC TRANSCRIPTIONS WITH NOTES AND TABLATURE**

| | | |
|---|---|---|
| 00690949 | Rod Stewart Guitar Anthology | $19.99 |
| 00690021 | Sting – Fields of Gold | $19.95 |
| 00690689 | Story of the Year – Page Avenue | $19.95 |
| 00690520 | Styx Guitar Collection | $19.95 |
| 00120081 | Sublime | $19.95 |
| 00690992 | Sublime – Robbin' the Hood | $19.99 |
| 00690519 | SUM 41 – All Killer No Filler | $19.95 |
| 00691072 | Best of Supertramp | $22.99 |
| 00690994 | Taylor Swift | $22.99 |
| 00690993 | Taylor Swift – Fearless | $22.99 |
| 00691063 | Taylor Swift – Speak Now | $22.99 |
| 00690767 | Switchfoot – The Beautiful Letdown | $19.95 |
| 00690830 | System of a Down – Hypnotize | $19.95 |
| 00690531 | System of a Down – Toxicity | $19.95 |
| 00694824 | Best of James Taylor | $16.95 |
| 00694887 | Best of Thin Lizzy | $19.95 |
| 00690871 | Three Days Grace – One-X | $19.95 |
| 00690891 | 30 Seconds to Mars – A Beautiful Lie | $19.95 |
| 00690030 | Toad the Wet Sprocket | $19.95 |
| 00690233 | The Merle Travis Collection | $19.99 |
| 00690683 | Robin Trower – Bridge of Sighs | $19.95 |
| 00699191 | U2 – Best of: 1980-1990 | $19.95 |
| 00690732 | U2 – Best of: 1990-2000 | $19.95 |
| 00690894 | U2 – 18 Singles | $19.95 |
| 00690775 | U2 – How to Dismantle an Atomic Bomb | $22.95 |
| 00690997 | U2 – No Line on the Horizon | $19.99 |
| 00690039 | Steve Vai – Alien Love Secrets | $24.95 |
| 00690172 | Steve Vai – Fire Garden | $24.95 |
| 00660137 | Steve Vai – Passion & Warfare | $24.95 |
| 00690881 | Steve Vai – Real Illusions: Reflections | $24.95 |
| 00694904 | Steve Vai – Sex and Religion | $24.95 |
| 00690392 | Steve Vai – The Ultra Zone | $19.95 |
| 00690024 | Stevie Ray Vaughan – Couldn't Stand the Weather | $19.95 |
| 00690370 | Stevie Ray Vaughan and Double Trouble – The Real Deal: Greatest Hits Volume 2 | $22.95 |
| 00690116 | Stevie Ray Vaughan – Guitar Collection | $24.95 |
| 00660136 | Stevie Ray Vaughan – In Step | $19.95 |
| 00694879 | Stevie Ray Vaughan – In the Beginning | $19.95 |
| 00660058 | Stevie Ray Vaughan – Lightnin' Blues '83-'87 | $24.95 |
| 00690036 | Stevie Ray Vaughan – Live Alive | $24.95 |
| 00694835 | Stevie Ray Vaughan – The Sky Is Crying | $22.95 |
| 00690025 | Stevie Ray Vaughan – Soul to Soul | $19.95 |
| 00690015 | Stevie Ray Vaughan – Texas Flood | $19.95 |
| 00690772 | Velvet Revolver – Contraband | $22.95 |
| 00690132 | The T-Bone Walker Collection | $19.95 |
| 00694789 | Muddy Waters – Deep Blues | $24.95 |
| 00690071 | Weezer (The Blue Album) | $19.95 |
| 00690516 | Weezer (The Green Album) | $19.95 |
| 00690286 | Weezer – Pinkerton | $19.95 |
| 00691046 | Weezer – Rarities Edition | $22.99 |
| 00690447 | Best of the Who | $24.95 |
| 00694970 | The Who – Definitive Guitar Collection: A-E | $24.95 |
| 00694971 | The Who – Definitive Guitar Collection F-Li | $24.95 |
| 00694972 | The Who – Definitive Guitar Collection: Lo-R | $24.95 |
| 00690672 | Best of Dar Williams | $19.95 |
| 00691017 | Wolfmother – Cosmic Egg | $22.99 |
| 00690319 | Stevie Wonder – Some of the Best | $17.95 |
| 00690596 | Best of the Yardbirds | $19.95 |
| 00690844 | Yellowcard – Lights and Sounds | $19.95 |
| 00690916 | The Best of Dwight Yoakam | $19.95 |
| 00690904 | Neil Young – Harvest | $29.99 |
| 00690905 | Neil Young – Rust Never Sleeps | $19.99 |
| 00690443 | Frank Zappa – Hot Rats | $19.95 |
| 00690624 | Frank Zappa and the Mothers of Invention – One Size Fits All | $22.99 |
| 00690623 | Frank Zappa – Over-Nite Sensation | $22.99 |
| 00690589 | ZZ Top – Guitar Anthology | $24.95 |
| 00690960 | ZZ Top Guitar Classics | $19.99 |

HAL•LEONARD® CORPORATION
7777 W. BLUEMOUND RD. P.O. BOX 13819 MILWAUKEE, WI 53213

Complete songlists and more at **www.halleonard.com**
Prices, contents, and availability subject to change without notice.

# Hal•Leonard GUITAR PLAY-ALONG

**INCLUDES TAB**

This series will help you play your favorite songs quickly and easily. Just follow the tab and listen to the CD to hear how the guitar should sound, and then play along using the separate backing tracks. Mac or PC users can also slow down the tempo without changing pitch by using the CD in their computer. The melody and lyrics are included in the book so that you can sing or simply follow along.

**1. ROCK**
00699570 .................... $16.99

**2. ACOUSTIC**
00699569 .................... $16.95

**3. HARD ROCK**
00699573 .................... $16.95

**4. POP/ROCK**
00699571 .................... $16.99

**5. MODERN ROCK**
00699574 .................... $16.99

**6. '90S ROCK**
00699572 .................... $16.99

**7. BLUES**
00699575 .................... $16.95

**8. ROCK**
00699585 .................... $14.99

**9. PUNK ROCK**
00699576 .................... $14.95

**10. ACOUSTIC**
00699586 .................... $16.95

**11. EARLY ROCK**
0699579 .................... $14.95

**12. POP/ROCK**
00699587 .................... $14.95

**13. FOLK ROCK**
00699581 .................... $15.99

**14. BLUES ROCK**
00699582 .................... $16.95

**15. R&B**
00699583 .................... $14.95

**16. JAZZ**
00699584 .................... $15.95

**17. COUNTRY**
00699588 .................... $15.95

**18. ACOUSTIC ROCK**
00699577 .................... $15.95

**19. SOUL**
00699578 .................... $14.99

**20. ROCKABILLY**
00699580 .................... $14.95

**21. YULETIDE**
00699602 .................... $14.95

**22. CHRISTMAS**
00699600 .................... $15.95

**23. SURF**
00699635 .................... $14.95

**24. ERIC CLAPTON**
00699649 .................... $17.99

**25. LENNON & McCARTNEY**
00699642 .................... $16.99

**26. ELVIS PRESLEY**
00699643 .................... $14.95

**27. DAVID LEE ROTH**
00699645 .................... $16.95

**28. GREG KOCH**
00699646 .................... $14.95

**29. BOB SEGER**
00699647 .................... $15.99

**30. KISS**
00699644 .................... $16.99

**31. CHRISTMAS HITS**
00699652 .................... $14.95

**32. THE OFFSPRING**
00699653 .................... $14.95

**33. ACOUSTIC CLASSICS**
00699656 .................... $16.95

**34. CLASSIC ROCK**
00699658 .................... $16.95

**35. HAIR METAL**
00699660 .................... $16.95

**36. SOUTHERN ROCK**
00699661 .................... $16.95

**37. ACOUSTIC METAL**
00699662 .................... $16.95

**38. BLUES**
00699663 .................... $16.95

**39. '80S METAL**
00699664 .................... $16.99

**40. INCUBUS**
00699668 .................... $17.95

**41. ERIC CLAPTON**
00699669 .................... $16.95

**42. 2000S ROCK**
00699670 .................... $16.99

**43. LYNYRD SKYNYRD**
00699681 .................... $17.95

**44. JAZZ**
00699689 .................... $14.99

**45. TV THEMES**
00699718 .................... $14.95

**46. MAINSTREAM ROCK**
00699722 .................... $16.95

**47. HENDRIX SMASH HITS**
00699723 .................... $19.95

**48. AEROSMITH CLASSICS**
00699724 .................... $17.99

**49. STEVIE RAY VAUGHAN**
00699725 .................... $17.99

**51. ALTERNATIVE '90S**
00699727 .................... $14.99

**52. FUNK**
00699728 .................... $14.95

**53. DISCO**
00699729 .................... $14.99

**54. HEAVY METAL**
00699730 .................... $14.95

**55. POP METAL**
00699731 .................... $14.95

**56. FOO FIGHTERS**
00699749 .................... $15.99

**57. SYSTEM OF A DOWN**
00699751 .................... $14.95

**58. BLINK-182**
00699772 .................... $14.95

**60. 3 DOORS DOWN**
00699774 .................... $14.95

**61. SLIPKNOT**
00699775 .................... $16.99

**62. CHRISTMAS CAROLS**
00699798 .................... $12.95

**63. CREEDENCE CLEARWATER REVIVAL**
00699802 .................... $16.99

**64. OZZY OSBOURNE**
00699803 .................... $16.99

**65. THE DOORS**
00699806 .................... $16.99

**66. THE ROLLING STONES**
00699807 .................... $16.95

**67. BLACK SABBATH**
0699808 .................... $16.99

**68. PINK FLOYD – DARK SIDE OF THE MOON**
00699809 .................... $16.99

**69. ACOUSTIC FAVORITES**
00699810 .................... $14.95

**70. OZZY OSBOURNE**
00699805 .................... $16.99

**71. CHRISTIAN ROCK**
00699824 .................... $14.95

**72. ACOUSTIC '90s**
00699827 .................... $14.95

**73. BLUESY ROCK**
00699829 .................... $16.99

**74. PAUL BALOCHE**
00699831 .................... $14.95